'The little house of the Sacred Heart'

A Providential Gift

# THE ACADEMY
# OF THE SACRED HEART
# AT GRAND COTEAU

## *200 Years and Counting...*

## DARLENE SMITH

Connor,
    With gratitude for your
love and support of your family —
And for reminding me of my dad,
your great-grandpa Nick —
                With love —
                Aunt Darlene
        3-24-22

**Acadian House**
PUBLISHING
Lafayette, Louisiana

Copyright © 2021 by Darlene Smith

All rights reserved, including the right to reproduce this book or portions thereof in any form whatsoever. For information, contact Acadian House Publishing, P.O. Box 52247, Lafayette, Louisiana 70505, or via e-mail: info@acadianhouse.com.

Library of Congress Control Number: 2021945032

ISBN 10: 1-7352641-1-3
ISBN 13: 978-1-7352641-1-0

- ♦ Published by Acadian House Publishing, Lafayette, Louisiana
  (Edited by Trent Angers; editorial assistance and research by Madison Louviere)
- ♦ Design and pre-press production by Allison Nassans
- ♦ Printed by Walsworth Printing, Marceline, Missouri

*The 200-year history of the Academy of the Sacred Heart in Grand Coteau, Louisiana, is illustrative of the hard work and dedication of so many strong, committed women who deserve great thanks for the treasure that is the Academy. This commemorative book is a tribute to them.*

# *Steadfast in Our Mission*
## ~ A Message from the Head of School ~

Upon reflection, it's difficult to imagine life 200 years ago in 1821. A time before the age of indoor plumbing and electricity, of cars, planes, and space travel; before penicillin and antibiotics; before Vietnam, the World Wars, and even the Civil War, our country was in its adolescence, with uncharted wilderness and young American citizens emblazoned to forge their paths and create new lives and new frontiers on our American soil. It was a time of great difficulty and challenges, but also of great triumphs of vision and optimism and hope for the future, of perseverance and willpower, and of great faith and powerful conviction.

Two hundred years ago, St. Philippine Duchesne, at the urging of our foundress, St. Madeleine Sophie Barat, defied all odds and set out to follow God's calling and bring education for young women to our new America. Braving the treacherous transatlantic journey and then the challenges of new cultures, new languages, new climates and diseases, St. Philippine and her brave RSCJs persevered, and our first American Sacred Heart school opened in Missouri. A short time later, Mother Eugénie Audé and Sister Mary Layton journeyed even farther south, to the swamps of Louisiana. With the donation of land and a farmhouse from Mrs. Charles Smith along with the significant and continued contributions of enslaved persons, the doors of the Academy of the Sacred Heart in Grand Coteau opened October 5, 1821.

Over the next two centuries, through pandemics, wars, and economic depressions, the Academy doors have remained open and generations of bold, faith-filled, intelligent, difference-making women have joined the esteemed ranks of Coteau alumnae. A badge of honor, our alumnae carry their love for Coteau, for the Five Goals, for our founding saints, and for their bond of sisterhood with them throughout their lives. These girls were raised under our stately Oaks, and as many will tell you, a Sacred Heart alum is always set apart in the crowd for her confidence, intelligence, and compassion.

As we celebrate our bicentennial and all who have gone before us, we honor their legacy and our history. We remain steadfast in our Mission and our Goals and hold on to that same tenacity, courage, and confidence, as we look to the future and our next two hundred years.

In the Heart of the Lord,

*Yvonne Sandoz Adler*

Yvonne Sandoz Adler, Ph.D.
Head of School

## Note on Sources

One of the primary sources used to tell this story is the *House Journal 1821-1884*, which was translated from French to English by Sr. Katharine Townsend, RSCJ, in the 1970s. The *House Journal* is written in the style and vocabulary of the 19th century, and the translated material from the *Journal* used in this book is quoted directly.

Language and terms which might be considered demeaning today are presented exactly as they were written in the *Journal*. Additionally, some of the language to describe different events might today be considered old-fashioned and too flowery, yet much of it is eloquently literary.

Other sources include the excellent RSCJ website and the *Lettres Annuelles*, parts of which were painstakingly translated by Dr. Anna (Laurie) Servaes for use in this book. The library at the Academy in Grand Coteau contains many books and documents that help to tell this amazing story. While they are available to the casual reader and to the inquisitive scholar, those sources are for perusal only in the ASH library.

The Society of the Sacred Heart Archives, United States-Canada Province, in St. Louis, Missouri, were invaluable to me. I could not have found many of the resources used to construct this history without the assistance of the archivists, Sr. Carolyn Osiek, RSCJ, and Sr. Mary Lou Gavan, RSCJ. Particularly valuable were the letters of General Nathaniel Banks and the Attestation of Mary Wilson.

Photos used in this book are courtesy of the Society of the Sacred Heart Archives, United States-Canada Province, and the Academy of the Sacred Heart in Grand Coteau, unless otherwise noted.

# Foreword

Turning the corner to the Academy of the Sacred Heart one autumn day in 1978, I had no idea that I would spend the best years of my professional life at the Academy. But somehow I knew that I would work there someday.

Three years later, I began teaching III and IV Prep students in a school with an administration that valued innovation in education and appreciated my efforts to engage students in a variety of subjects and activities. I was blessed to teach there for 31 years, from 1981 until my retirement in 2012. Even after all these years of retirement, I still describe myself as a Sacred Heart teacher, one with a deep appreciation for the gift of the Academy.

So to Sr. Lucie Nordmann, RSCJ, and Sr. Sharon Karam, RSCJ, I say thank you for taking a chance on me and hiring me to teach English and literature. I hope in some small way that this book expresses my gratitude for the privilege of being a Sacred Heart teacher.

The Academy has always met obstacles and overcome them throughout its 200 years. It is my fondest hope that the Schools of the Sacred Heart will continue to meet the many challenges of educating young women and men in a world that is often at odds with the guiding principles of Sacred Heart and its Goals and Criteria. May it see many more years of teaching and inspiring the young people entrusted to its care.

*– Darlene Smith*

# Table of Contents

*Message from the Head of School* ................................................................ iv

*Note on Sources* ........................................................................................ vi

*Foreword* ................................................................................................ vii

*Introduction* ........................................................................................... 10

## Part I –
### Early History of the Academy of the Sacred Heart (1821-1899) — 11

1. The Birth of a Legacy ......................................................................... 13
2. From Small Beginnings ...................................................................... 17
3. The Campus Expands .......................................................................... 24
4. The Jesuits Settle in Grand Coteau .................................................... 29
5. Slavery in Antebellum Times ............................................................. 31
6. Civil War and the Academy ............................................................... 36
7. The Miracle of Grand Coteau ............................................................ 42
8. Educating a Newly Freed People ....................................................... 46
9. *Mater Admirabilis!* ........................................................................ 52
10. The 19th Century Comes to an End .................................................. 55

## Part II –
### The 20th Century (1900-1999) — 57

11. A New Century ................................................................................. 59
12. Growth of 'The House of Grand Coteau' ........................................... 62
13. Normal School and College of the Sacred Heart ............................... 74
14. The World War II Years .................................................................... 78
15. The Impact of Vatican II ................................................................... 82

**Part III –**
**Onward to the 21st Century** ................................................................ **85**

16. Sacred Heart GOALS and CRITERIA ............................................. 87
17. Toward a Noble Future ................................................................... 93

**Part IV –**
**Traditions, Treasures & People of Faith** ...................................... **97**

18. Traditions, Customs & Activities .................................................. 99
19. The Saints of Sacred Heart ........................................................ 107
20. Women of Faith and Influence .................................................... 117

*Glossary* ............................................................................................... 139

*Timeline* ............................................................................................... 142

Appendix 1 - The Great Flood of 1927 ............................................... 144

Appendix 2 - Hymns, Prayers and Poems of the Schools of the Sacred Heart ............. 147

Appendix 3 - Treasured Recipes from the Coteau Family ................... 152

Appendix 4 - Administrative Leaders ................................................. 157

Appendix 5 - To Become a Religious of the Sacred Heart ................. 162

Appendix 6 - Giving Opportunities .................................................... 163

*Sources* ................................................................................................ 165

*References* ........................................................................................... 167

*Index* .................................................................................................... 170

*Contact Information* ............................................................................ 175

*Photo and Art Credits* ......................................................................... 177

*Acknowledgements* ............................................................................. 178

*About the Author* ................................................................................ 179

# Introduction

For the first-time visitor to the Academy of the Sacred Heart in Grand Coteau, Louisiana – indeed for any visitor – a pleasant and welcoming vista awaits. Upon turning the curve toward the school, one sees the beauty and serenity of verdant fields anchored by rows of pines and oaks, grazing cattle and horses, and a canopy of trees arching over the road leading to the front of the school. Across the road facing the main building is an alley of majestic oaks known as Oakdale. The grounds are spectacular. And so is the story of the Academy.

Few businesses or institutions in south Louisiana are older than the Academy of the Sacred Heart, which has been operated by women and educating young ladies for two centuries and young men since 2006. ASH-Coteau, which has the distinction of being the longest continuously operating school in the Network of 150-plus Sacred Heart schools worldwide, was one of the pioneer educational ventures in the state. From its very beginning, the school reflected a diversified populace, which has continued over the years with students from Central America, Mexico, Europe, Africa, Australia, and Pacific Rim countries such as Japan and South Korea.

Founded in 1821 by the Society of the Religious of the Sacred Heart – RSCJ, *La Société du Sacré Cœur de Jésus* – the Academy not only has a legacy of high standards and achievement in education, but it also has a rich history encompassing hurricanes, fires, sickness, wars, and miracles.

# Part I

# Early History

## of the Academy of the Sacred Heart

## (1821-1899)

*"Founded on the rock of the Cross,
this house will withstand all storms."*

– St. Madeleine Sophie Barat, RSCJ

Chapter 1

# The Birth of a Legacy

In the early 1820s, Grand Coteau, Louisiana, was a small but thriving community where stagecoaches stopped to change horses, and travelers could stay at the local inn. There were businesses such as bakeries, a millinery shop, a blacksmith shop, general stores, and a post office.

It was fertile ground for schools and churches; indeed, its future would be shaped by religion. The establishment of the Society of the Sacred Heart novitiate and the Academy of the Sacred Heart here brought with it an international flavor that connected to Canada, Europe, and Latin America.

The Academy's story really starts in 1803, as the *House Journal* points out, when *"Charles Smith, a zealous Christian, and his wife, Mary Sentee of Pennsylvania, came to settle in Louisiana a short time after the United States took possession of this country (1803).... As both were hard-working and thrifty, they built up a considerable fortune, and bought a large amount of land, particularly in the prairie of Grand Coteau, which the Lord seems to have chosen in order to establish there His reign, and there take His delight. [Charles]... in union with his wife, conceived the project of building a church, and a school for Christian youth."* [1]

Charles Smith and his wife, Mary Sentee Smith, who had converted to Catholicism and was baptized in Opelousas, were generous benefactors of the Church and wished to devote much of their fortune to the spread of Catholicism in their section of the country.

Mr. Smith died unexpectedly on April 1, 1819, before the school was established; however, his will made clear that he gave everything to his wife:

*"Desiring to carry out her husband's project of the education of youth, she consulted Msgr. William Louis DuBourg, who had come to make his pastoral visit at Opelousas. Following his advice, she decided upon a congregation of women with whom she could retire at this time of her life, and fixed her choice on the Sacred Heart."* [2]

Mrs. Smith had generously offered a two-story, 55-foot Louisiana cypress French-colonial building, a property of 150 acres with three smaller houses, an enslaved family and money to begin a school.

Mother Philippine Duchesne, RSCJ, who was then in Missouri, considered the request of Monsignor DuBourg for a school in Louisiana. Subsequently, she *"sent to make this foundation of Grand Coteau, Mother Eugénie Audé and Sister Mary Laiton [more frequently spelled Layton], a co-adjutrix sister from Maryland."* [3] She submitted the plan in a letter to the Superior General, Madeleine Sophie Barat, writing:

*"Mother Audé is quite capable of governing a house. She has very good judgment,*

*prudence enough not to act impulsively, great zeal and firmness. Her appearance and conversation are attractive, she knows enough English to make herself easily understood by Americans, and above all, she has a love of her vocation which leaves nothing to be desired.*" [4]

Eugénie Audé, who was born on May 14, 1792, grew up in a peaceful, prosperous home high in the mountains of Savoy. It was fortunate that Eugénie lived in a province that was far ahead of others in the education of women; she, being rather precocious, benefited from an excellent education. In a time of revolution, her father, Etienne, embraced the republican form of government and later was appointed to the Civil Tribunal of his district. During this time of peace as Napoleon was growing his empire, Eugénie trained for presentation at court. She learned to sing, play a musical instrument, and to write verses. She practiced sitting down gracefully, crossing a room, putting on and removing gloves, and taking a gentleman's hand prettily. However, three months after her beloved father's death, in 1815, she renounced this privileged world and entered the Society of the Sacred Heart in service of God.

She, like Mother Philippine Duchesne, longed to go to the New World and spread the love of Christ by establishing schools for girls. Finally, in 1818, Philippine and Eugénie set sail for America, accompanied by three other missionaries, including Marguerite Manteau, who later spent the last years of her life at Grand Coteau, where she died in 1841. After long weeks at sea with the pervasive smells and sounds of the small ship *Rebecca*, they finally sighted American land and slowly made their way to New Orleans. After setting foot in Louisiana, Mother Duchesne knelt and kissed the muddy ground, and, since no one was looking, encouraged the others to kiss it, too. While waiting for passage to St. Louis, they learned rudimentary English and stayed with the Ursuline nuns, who entreated them to open a school in New Orleans. After a month of waiting, and dressed in light cotton because of the heat, they boarded the boat to Missouri.

Upon reaching their destination, Mother Audé worked alongside her colleagues to establish a school – or foundation – in St. Charles, Missouri. Somehow, with limited resources, they were able to open a free school on September 14, 1818, for six pupils, and shortly thereafter a boarding school on October 1.

Later, in a letter to the Society's foundress, Madeleine Sophie Barat, RSCJ, Mother Duchesne noted that Eugénie Audé would make a fine future superior, and in 1821 chose her to establish the new Louisiana foundation that was being endowed by the Smiths. It was also hoped that the warmer climate of Louisiana would be better for Mother Audé's declining health. As Mother Duchesne explained to Mother Barat, "*Last year, we feared we might lose her.*" [5]

After the long trip from St. Louis down the Mississippi River, Mother Audé and Sister Layton traveled on *Le Rapide* as far as Plaquemines, Louisiana, where they were deposited onto a very muddy shore. They trudged through the mire for about 15 minutes before reaching an inn. They stayed there for two nights, a stay made unpleasant by spiders and rowdy, quarreling neighbors. Mother Audé wrote descriptively that they "*lodged in a small room tapestried in spider-webs.*" [6]

Naturally, they were happy to leave, and they journeyed overland in oxcarts until they were 20 miles from their destination, the little village of Grand Coteau. On a hot late-summer day, accompanied by a small party of men travelling in the same direction, they gamely ventured on, completing their journey on horseback.

Eugénie was not a practiced rider. She wrote in her letter to Mother Barat :

"*I was very embarrassed, mounting and trying to keep my seat on the courser whose mane kept me from falling off more than once.*" [7]

Anyone who has experienced or even just heard about the hot, humid summers in south Louisiana can appreciate the determination and courage of these intrepid women who were relatively new to the South.

Upon arrival in Grand Coteau on Aug-

*Mother Rose Philippine Duchesne made the trans-Atlantic journey between Europe and North America to spend many years of service in the cause of Catholic education.*

ust 25, 1821, they lodged for three weeks in the home of Mrs. Smith, since "*the little house of the Sacred Heart*" [8] had not yet been completed. Their future dwelling was made of wood and had two long galleries; it had been recently painted but it had no furniture. The days that followed their occupation of the house would bring some furniture and they would begin to get things in order.

" *...Filled with a holy impatience to begin the work of the Lord, [Mother Audé] went to establish herself there as well as she could. She took up her lodging in a little room, the door of which she blocked with a table during the night.... As trouble with her feet hindered her from walking, she dragged herself on her hands and knees from room to room, in order to advance the work.*" [9]

She had had a serious eye infection, which the doctor treated by blistering her feet to relieve the inflammation. As a result, she was temporarily crippled and could scarcely drag herself. Prayer and the ministrations of Mrs. Smith eventually restored the patient to health. Until conditions improved, Sr. Layton and Mother Audé contended with sleeping on dirt floors while wrapped in sheets, no glass in the windows, little furniture, and

*Mrs. Charles Smith's donation to the Society of the Sacred Heart included this 55-foot long, 2-story wood frame house, which served as the original schoolhouse and convent. She also donated three smaller houses, as well as 150 acres of land.*

plenty of Louisiana creatures for company, particularly mosquitoes.

Despite frequent hunger and exhaustion, the two nuns labored to secure furnishings, locks for doors, provisions for themselves and their pupils, as well as school materials and altar items. More than material hardship and constant work, the deprivation of the services of priests for Masses was keenly felt. For months at a time there were no priests available.

The fledgling enterprise actually had three purposes: a school for girls, a convent for the nuns, and a novitiate to train young women to become members of the Society of the Sacred Heart. From 1821 to 1825, novices were trained at Grand Coteau before the novitiate was moved to St. Michael's, another small Sacred Heart school and convent on the Mississippi, upriver from New Orleans. Years later, in 1848, Mother Maria Cutts, RSCJ, brought the novitiate back to Grand Coteau and it continued there until 1896.

*Le Rapide provided transport down the Mississippi River to Plaquemine, Louisiana, for Mother Audé and Sister Layton on their initial voyage to Grand Coteau.*

# Chapter 2

# From Small Beginnings

During the week of October 5, 1821, eight pupils provided the initial roster of the school, known officially as the Institute for the Education of Young Ladies.

They were 15-year-old Pennsylvanian Mary Sentee; from New Orleans came Louise Montbrain, Laura Baron, and Elisa Baron; and from Opelousas were Félonise Poiret, Zelia Rousseau, Gadrate Rousseau, and Paméla Moor. The youngest student was only six years old.

Daily prayer, Bible history, religion, French and English grammar, penmanship, literature, composition, chronology of history, and music were integral elements of their activities and studies. They also learned to sew and embroider and to manage the housekeeping of a large plantation. It was called **The Practical Teaching of Domestic Science**. Various religious celebrations, such as the *Fête Dieu*, Renewal of Vows, Mass (when a priest was available), Vespers, feast days of saints, and First Communion were prayerfully and enthusiastically observed.

Pupils lived at the school and attended classes taught by Mother Audé, the new school's first Mother Superior, who also cooked for them and managed the boarding school. Though Mother Audé had never cooked before, she enjoyed the challenge of providing good and nutritious food for the pupils. A staple of their diet was Indian corn; it could be used for spoon-bread, mush, porridge, and an early version of grits known as *petit gru*. Game from the woods and fish were treats not often on the menu. In fact, the stock of provisions was monotonously plain.

Sr. Layton did the other work of the school and kept it as clean as she could. Early on, they "*...received, gratis, a young girl from New Orleans ... who took care of the lesser business of the house...,*" the *House Journal* noted. [1]

In these early years, because travel was so difficult and uncertain, the school year covered eleven months. Summer vacation began toward the end of August with *rentrée* usually beginning at the start of October. The pupils were allowed to go home at Easter, but there were no Christmas or Mardi Gras holidays. Instead, during the Christmas season, the girls' families would gather at the school for *congés* and Christmas liturgies and celebrations. The families and friends came from the area plantations in carriages drawn by well-groomed horses and driven by liveried coachmen.

By 1822, more Religious and postulants arrived to assist at the fledging school. Including the newly arrived postulants, the Community now had eight members, and the school of eight pupils would laughingly say, "*Each one of us has her own Mistress!*" [2] They all participated in a moving liturgy on June 6, 1822, called *Fête Dieu*. "*We had the*

*The land upon which the Academy is built is characterized by a natural, even primordial beauty that has inspired artists, writers and photographers for generations.*

*procession before Mass at which several persons assisted. The Repository was tastefully arranged in the woods back of the house. This was the first ceremony of this kind in this quarter of the country."* [3]

On April 1, 1822, Mother Anna Xavier Murphy, RSCJ, arrived at Grand Coteau. For nearly the next 15 years the history of the school became one with the life story of Mother Xavier, whose vocation was to be a missionary for Christ. Leaving her native Ireland and entering the Paris novitiate in May of 1820, she set out for Louisiana just weeks after making her first vows, on November 6, 1821. Mother Barat, recommending her, noted that she spoke perfect English, but had no artistic talent and would need guidance with the Plan of Studies. She was intelligent, courageous, persevering, and enthusiastic and had the making *"of a valiant missionary."* [4] Her letter to Mother Barat recounting her experiences during the 55-day voyage to America captures her sense of wonder and enthusiasm for adventure:

*...The sight of that limitless expanse [of the open sea] roused in me a sensation I can never describe, but it was very delightful.... I was sick at times but never the least bit afraid.... Sunrise and sunset were gorgeous, and then there was moonrise or the starry heavens lighting the ocean with a glint of silver.* [5]

The first RSCJ to be finally professed in the New World, Mother Xavier made her final vows May 14, 1822, with Msgr. DuBourg officiating in the chapel of Grand Coteau. She assumed her duties as teacher and assistant in the boarding school with alacrity. By this time, there were 17 boarders with five or six more expected, and a free school was opened in a new log house.

But the scarcity of priests was a privation keenly felt by the Religious. Mother Xavier, as the scribe, often had to write in the *House Journal* the words "No Mass," which distressed the Community greatly.

With the school just eight months in operation, Mother Xavier had arrived at a time of stability, due to good organization and an institution completely free from debt. In the workshops, hide-seated chairs, wooden beds and dried-moss mattresses were produced. Desks and benches had been installed in classrooms, and study halls contained books, globes, and other school supplies in abundance. The pupils were clad in uniforms, and regular exams were inaugurated.

Because Louisiana was proving to be a productive area for the Society's mission, another school and convent were planned for a promising spot on the banks of the Mississippi River known today as Convent, Louisiana. It was decided that Mother Eugénie Audé was to be the foundress of this second Sacred Heart school. She left Grand Coteau on March 21, 1825, with plans for the new foundation.

Her colleague, Mother Anna Xavier Murphy, would become the second Superior at Grand Coteau. It was a responsibility that was at first a great anxiety to Mother Xavier. She did not think she was capable of fulfilling the duties and responsibilities of this new office. One of her first difficulties was adjusting to the reduction of the Religious to just five members while still having to carry out the necessary work until reinforcements from France would arrive in 1827. One of the new personnel was Mother Louise Dorival, RSCJ, who would serve as assistant to Mother Xavier.

Religious assistance came from the friendship formed between Mother Xavier and Bishop Rosati, whose visit was the outstanding event recorded in the convent annals for 1828. His wise counsel and encouragement from 1828 until her death in 1836 filled Mother Xavier with confidence.

During her tenure, she welcomed more Religious and pupils; oversaw the construction of a new brick building with the now-iconic facade, a bakery, and brick quarters for the farm workers; and laid plans for the chapel. She also began the beautification of the grounds, planting trees and designing the formal garden; engaged two Frenchmen and an Italian music master, who became the first music teachers at Grand Coteau; and even acquired two pianos. She successfully took precautions to spare the Coteau

*St. Michael's was another Academy of the Sacred Heart, founded in the 1820s and located upriver from New Orleans. In its heyday, it served as a school and convent and, for a while, as a novitiate.*

community from the ravages of the Asiatic cholera epidemic that was sweeping through Louisiana. And, very significantly, she campaigned in earnest for the establishment of a Jesuit college in the immediate area.

Perhaps the most poignant of her achievements was her relationship with Frank Hawkins, an enslaved person of African descent who was acquired in July of 1823. She found in Frank a diligent, hard-working young man, to whom she gave great responsibilities. Eventually, she knew him well enough to see that he had grown increasingly unhappy. Having won his confidence, she encouraged him to share his story.

He explained that he had been married and was sold away by his previous master, Theodore Mudd, a Catholic planter in Maryland. Frank had been forcibly separated from his wife, Jenny, with whom he already had a son, Francis Jr. Now Jenny was living on a plantation several miles away, and Frank sometimes was able to be with her. In September of 1823 Jenny gave birth to their daughter, Arminta, who did not survive, and later gave birth to her second son, Benjamin.

Mother Xavier united the family on December 4, 1829, by purchasing Jenny and her two sons and bringing them to Grand Coteau. On his deathbed in 1842, Frank expressed his willingness to die because he was eager to see Mother Xavier again in heaven.

From the beginning of her time in Louisiana, Mother Xavier had often endured fevers, perhaps malaria, and then recovered enough to carry out her many duties. But the fever that struck her in August of 1836 lingered, caused a trembling in the hand, weakened her body, and prompted the local doctor – *"versed in the medical ignorance of the day"* [6] – to prescribe a series of blistering plasters. It was a cruel treatment that left her further weakened and in great pain, which she bore with patience and faith.

A priest was summoned on September 3 to administer the Last Sacraments, and her fellow Religious gathered around her bed, keeping a vigil until her death at midnight, September 6, 1836. Her passing was an immense loss not only to the Religious but also to the extended community of Grand Coteau. Within a few days of her death, her faithful nurse, Mother Rose Elder, also died of the same disease, on September 21. They are buried near each other in the cemetery on the Academy grounds.

Also noteworthy among these new 1822 arrivals was Mother Carmelite Landry, RSCJ, of LaFourche (located in present-day Lafourche Parish), who became one of the first "Cajun" nuns, and who greatly assisted Mother Xavier. Theirs is a story of devotion to God, faithfulness to mission, and servitude to the works of the Lord. The two worked together at Coteau for many years, and when Carmelite died, in January of 1852, she was buried next to her beloved mentor and friend, Mother Xavier. The *House Journal* records a moving tribute to her upon her death.

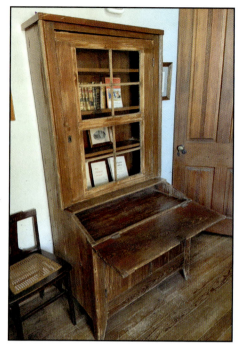

*This desk, on display in the school's museum, was used by Mother Duchesne when she visited the Academy in Grand Coteau.*

"*She* [Carmelite Landry] *was born in LaFourche in 1794, of a patriarchal family which had migrated from Canada to escape the dangers to Faith which menaced them when their native land fell under English domination.... She died at the moment when Mother Lévèque, reciting beside her the prayers of the agonizing, invoked the choir of virgins to come forth to meet her. After death, her features, which had been entirely altered by the horrible sufferings of her agony, took on again their former serenity.... It was difficult to draw oneself away from gazing upon this body, which seemed to repose so sweetly in the arms of God. Her age was 57 years and ten months....*" [7]

Hers was a life of devoted obedience and humility. Always an example to the young girls she knew, Mother Landry allowed nothing to weaken her vocation, and "*Her death was the evening of a beautiful soul.*" [8]

The most notable arrival in 1822 was Mother Philippine Duchesne. Wanting to visit the new establishment in Louisiana, she made the arduous trip from Missouri to Grand Coteau to visit her fellow Religious and to make new appointments. She found the house in Grand Coteau to be charming, well-established and free from debt. She noted: "*The chapel is pretty and devotional, the sacristy well supplied with sacred vessels, thanks to the generosity of several priests.*" [9]

*From Small Beginnings* **23**

Her arrival was the cause of much joy for the Community, and at a reception for her she was welcomed in an address by 13-year-old Mary Ann Hardey, one of the first pupils enrolled, a young lady who was to become one of its most illustrious alumnae.

But Mother Duchesne was distressed to witness the unhealthy physical state of the nuns. Mother Audé was physically exhausted, Sister Layton was ill again, Mother Xavier carried a slight temperature, and Sister Gerard, a novice, was exceedingly frail. Only Sister Landry was in a healthy state. Mother Duchesne was so impressed by her that she changed Sister Landry's status from coadjutrix sister to a choir religious.

The school community, including the 17 pupils, were happy to celebrate Mother Duchesne's 53rd birthday with her on August 29. Five days later she began the arduous trip home. But it was a journey fraught with delay and grave illness. Many fellow passengers on the riverboat were struck with yellow fever. Mother Duchesne also became dangerously ill and was left in a small upriver town where kind strangers provided shelter and care until she could continue the trip. She did not arrive in Florissant, Missouri, until November 20, 1822.

In 1823, there was widespread illness accompanied by economic distress throughout the region, but the house in Grand Coteau was spared much of the suffering. However, it did experience some devastation as a result of the hurricane of September 14. It tore trees from the ground and knocked down fences, creating much destruction. But the spirit prevailed and classes continued.

That same month the First Medallion was presented to Zelia Rousseau, whose great-granddaughter would be Sister Odéide Mouton, RSCJ, who would serve at various Sacred Heart schools and would spend her retirement at Grand Coteau from 1970 to 1985. A member of the illustrious and historically important Louisiana Mouton family, Sr. Mouton is buried in the cemetery on the campus.

The school's reputation for excellence was spreading throughout the area. An 1823 edition of the *Gazette de Opelousas* praised "*the boarding school at Grand Coteau… which offered a program of study previously unavailable in the region … for young ladies.*" [10] It was also noted that Catholic and non-Catholic were welcome, and there was no attempt at coercion toward a certain preference "in the matter of religion." [11]

*Sr. Odéide Mouton was a descendant of a member of the Academy's first class of students. She was also the great-aunt of a former headmistress of the Academy, Sr. Carolyn Mouton. This painting of the elder Sr. Mouton is displayed prominently in the Academy.*

# Chapter 3

# The Campus Expands

As the school grew, so did the need for more room. In 1830, a new brick building was begun by William Moore. He used Louisiana cypress for all of the wood in the building, and the bricks were made from clay dug from the brick pit that is now called *Lac Argile* on the school campus.

The first brick was laid on September 30 by Mr. Louis Lovallier from Opelousas. Then *"Each of our pupils laid a brick, and a paper (naming St. Joseph the protector of this foundation, and giving the date) was carefully placed in the corner-stone of the house."* [1]

The contracts in the convent archives record specifics of the construction project: *"100,000 good, merchantable bricks to be manufactured by George Schwing on the plantation and delivered within half a mile of the new site, on the first day of August, 1830, at the price of $10.00 per thousand and under the condition of $200.00 damages if late."* [2] Mother Xavier took possession of the new building on October 15, 1831, when the workmen gave her the keys.

Since the Academy provided a home for the Religious who worked there, it soon became necessary for a private cemetery to be opened. Mother Xavier had the cemetery made at the entrance to the woods, and the first to repose there was Mother Louise Dorival, who died July 11, 1832. From its earliest days, the cemetery became the final resting place for many of the Religious who have served the school. Several retired Religious have requested Grand Coteau for their burial place and many RSCJs are buried there.

In 1832-33, the Bishop's Cottage was completed. Mother Xavier wanted it to be built *"uniquement"* as the residence of Msgr. De Neckere when he came to visit. *"But so fragile are the plans of men – he would never see or occupy it."* [3]

Over the years, however, it did provide lodging for visiting clergy as well as for other guests. From 1838 to 1842, the cottage was occupied by a faculty family, Cornelia Connelly and her children, two of whom died while in Grand Coteau. Her husband, Pierce, taught English at the nearby Jesuit college, and Cornelia – who later would found the Society of the Holy Child Jesus – taught music at the Academy.

In 1835, an addition to the main brick building was erected, giving it a façade of 130 feet and a beautiful gallery. The first brick was laid by a Mr. Burgess, the husband of one of the former students, who expressed his wish for the success of the school. Then community members and students each laid a brick. Work progressed slowly because of bad weather and a cholera scare. When completed, the bricks were painted a creamy

*Construction of the iconic main building of the Academy of the Sacred Heart was begun in the fall of 1830, nine years after the school was founded.* **Above:** *Two of the floors were completed by the fall of 1831, and classes in the new building began soon thereafter.* **Below:** *The chapel wing (at left) was added in 1850, many years after construction of the main part of the building was completed. The chapel would have been built years earlier, but the 200,000 bricks intended for its construction were given away by Mother Superior Julie Bazire to the Jesuits, so they could build a college on their property a mile or so from the Academy.*

*Arched doorways in Greek Revival style add a touch of elegance to the design of the main building.*

*Customized ironwork and hand-blown glass from Paris add to the aesthetic appeal of the gallery. Much of the original glass remains today, after nearly two centuries.*

white to emulate the style of Hypolite Chretien's home in nearby Sunset, an estate called "Chretien Point."

Mother Xavier also planned a house kitchen, pantry, laundry, linen rooms and dormitories. A new bakery was put up some distance from the main buildings for fire safety, and brick cottages replaced the log cabins of the workers and their families.

The main building, where students have attended classes since the 1830s, has never been unoccupied. All of the woodwork, iron fasteners and other hardware and most of the window panes are of the original construction and of a type often found only in museums. When on the gallery, one can look for the "waves" in the original hand-blown glass from Paris (made around 1825), which is unlike the perfect machine-made glass of today. One can also find the "lines" of the bricks that indicate the various additions

*Pine Alley, leading to an entrance to the chapel, was planted in 1850, the same year in which the chapel was built.*

to the main building over the many decades of construction. The observer can also note the thickness of the windows and doorways and the genius of the Flemish bond brickwork.

Like so many antebellum buildings in the South, the Academy utilized the insulation properties of *bousillage* – a mixture usually of clay, deer or horse hair, and grass – and the high ceilings to help cool the building during the very hot and humid summers. The wide shaded gallery was designed for its cooling and aesthetic properties, as were the shutters for the many windows, also utilized for safety during hurricanes.

The formal garden, modeled after the elegant, but simple design of the French garden of Bishop Bossuet and noted for its geometrically patterned beds, was laid out in the mid-1830s under the direction of a Parisian gardener. The flowerbeds were delineated by bricks in the shapes of hearts, diamonds, stars, and circles. The grounds were planted with a variety of native plants and trees.

In 1850, the chapel wing was built on the west end of the main building, and Pine

*The cemetery on the grounds of the Academy was opened in the early 1830s. The first to be buried there was Mother Louise Dorival, who died of tuberculosis on July 11, 1832.*

*Sacred Heart nuns and students shared this home during the early years of the Academy. It is one of the four houses that Mrs. Charles Smith donated to the Society of the Sacred Heart to help with their educational mission.*

Alley, serving as a quiet and sometimes cool entryway to the chapel, was planted. Mother Xavier, who did not live to see its completion, had planned the chapel and scheduled it for construction in 1837. But it turned out that the 200,000 bricks made for the chapel were instead given by the new Mother Superior, Julie Bazire, RSCJ, to the Jesuits to construct their first building in Grand Coteau.

One of the oldest buildings to grace the grounds is the barn, which was built in 1854 with 10-foot arched openings and living quarters upstairs. The arched openings were later cut into square, bricked openings to allow hay wagons access to the storage space in the barn.

*A Sacred Heart nun ascends the stairs of her convent in the early days of the Academy, sometime in the mid to late 1800s.*

# Chapter 4

# The Jesuits Settle in Grand Coteau

Concurrent with the growth of construction on campus was the growth of the school and the novitiate. And with that came an increased need for the liturgical services of the clergy.

While the Academy grew academically in the early years of its existence, the *"privilege and joy of daily Mass"* [1] was often delayed for months as there were no priests regularly available in the area. Grand Coteau was not unique in its need for priests, and when the Jesuits sought property to start a college in south Louisiana, the towns of Iberville, Donaldsonville, and Grand Coteau vied as potential locations. At first, Donaldsonville was deemed to be a *"brilliant"* [2] location with many advantages, and early reports stated that it would be the site for the Jesuit establishment.

*"However, Fr. Point, still undecided, feels something which attracts him here (Grand Coteau)."* [3] During a visit to Donaldsonville, Fr. Nicholas Point received four letters from Mother Julie Bazire, the newly named superior of the convent, and these helped him to change his mind. After discussion with the other Jesuits and much prayer, he *"concluded that the Lord had spoken, and had declared Himself for Grand Coteau...."* [4]

In those letters, perhaps in order to secure the possibility of regular liturgies, Mother Julie Bazire had generously offered 200,000 bricks to the *"poor fathers, without funds, without fuel, and no wood for the framework of the new building."* [5] That promise and the generous offers made by the citizens of Grand Coteau helped Fr. Point to make his final decision. By July of 1837, those bricks *"were carted over a mile of cowpath to serve in the construction of the first building of St. Charles College in Grand Coteau."* [6] The land for the college was part of the generous gift of Mrs. Charles Smith, the well known benefactor of the Academy property, and was a most suitable and convenient location. On the Feast of the Apostles Peter and Paul, the Jesuit fathers planted the first three trees in their garden: a peach, a fig, and a pecan tree, gifts from Mother Bazire.

It was the start of a long, mutually beneficial relationship between the Jesuits and the nuns. The Religious of the Sacred Heart secured the promise of liturgical celebrations, especially Mass, First Communion, and retreats; the Jesuits were blessed with prayers and help from the nuns, especially in times of fires and other great needs. As early as 1838, when the fledgling college was supported by only 60 students, the Jesuit fathers suffered attacks from some of the locals:

*"...On all sides their enemies defamed them with such animosity, both in newspapers and in pamphlets, and aroused so many people against them, so much opposition and so many obstacles to their undertaking, that for a long time it was feared that the College would not survive."* [7]

Perhaps the fervent prayers and support of the nuns helped the enterprise survive

*Fr. John Francis Abbadie, S.J., was vice-rector of the Jesuits' brand new St. Charles College. He served the pastoral needs of the Academy as well as those of the local community at large. He died at age 86 in 1890 and is buried in the nearby Jesuit cemetery.*

those attacks.

The nuns were cloistered at that time, and the grateful Jesuits served as chaplains for the Religious and students of the school. And they would continue for nearly two centuries to minister to the Academy, often walking there under the alleys of oaks and pines that connect St. Charles College with the Academy. Today, this oak alley called "Oakdale" is the setting for the IV Academic (senior class) graduation liturgy and is often the location for senior pictures and weddings, as well as picnics and quiet meditation.

Among the Jesuits' many contributions to the Academy and its students was the establishment of the Sodality of the Children of Mary, in 1838. The effort was led by Fr. Point, rector of the Jesuits' newly opened college, a mile or so from the Academy.

When in the 1870s the Jesuits undertook the task of building a new church in Grand Coteau, the students and community at the Academy contributed with their time and treasures. One Community Fair, held on New Year's Day of 1876 – the United States' Centennial year – featured a pretty display of Academy goods sold at the fair, earning a sum of money that was subsequently donated to the church fund. Some of the items donated included dolls, watch-cases, shoes, artificial flowers and two woven baskets. The total earned from that fair was $2,500, a substantial amount. And it brought a gift from Fr. Olivier in return: ice cream!

The Sacred Heart Community would also rally to the aid of the Jesuits when their property was destroyed by fire in the early part of the twentieth century. In February of 1900, part of the College burned to the ground, and the loss of the beautiful library and its books was devastating, as the books were irreplaceable. Seven years later, the rest of the original building burned down as well. Many of the now-homeless priests sheltered at the Bishop's Cottage on the Academy's grounds. The nuns and students offered not only shelter, but also a multitude of prayers for the Jesuits.

*The Sodality of the Children of Mary was established at the Academy in 1838 by Fr. Nicholas Point, S.J., the rector of St. Charles College.*

# Chapter 5

# Slavery in Antebellum Times

One of the harsh realities during the early years of the United States was the legal institution of slavery, the buying and selling of human beings, in particular people of African descent.

In Louisiana, the *Code Noir* governed the behavior of the slave and the slave-owner, codifying laws, ordinances, decrees, and decisions concerning slavery. First drawn up by the French in 1724 and later amended by the Spanish Governor Antonio de Ulloa, the *Code Noir* normalized the legality of slavery and organized a society based on racist views.

Some of the mandates included religious practices, decreeing that the only religion and religious practices allowed were those of the Catholic Church and that slaves were to be baptized. The Code prohibited the union by marriage or cohabitation of blacks and whites, but stated that any children of such a union would be considered slaves.

Among the Code's other prohibitions: slaves could not be educated, could not gather in large groups, and were not allowed to carry weapons.

However, under the Code, enslaved persons were guaranteed a few rights. They were allowed to marry, their children younger than 14 could not be separated from their mothers, and they could not be forced to work on Sundays or religious holidays and were to be paid wages if they did work on those days. But the Code also allowed for recaptured runaway slaves to be whipped and/or branded, even to have an ear cut off as a warning to others. Having no legal rights, slaves who struck their masters could be killed. They were also not allowed to testify in court against their masters.

Despite the mandates of the Code, the administration of the *Code Noir* was usually determined by the slave-owners and planters; the courts seldom interfered with the slave-owners' authority.

It was into this culture that the Religious of the Sacred Heart arrived in 1821. During the antebellum years, the Academy, along with bishops, priests, and most of their students' families, owned enslaved persons. When the Jesuits founded their school in 1838, they and the Academy often shared enslaved persons. The first of these may have been a gift to the nuns from Mrs. Charles Smith, who held 25 enslaved persons on her property, and others would have accompanied the daughters of slave-holding families when those young women became pupils at the Academy. As early as 1821, Mother Audé received a young girl from New Orleans to help with "*the lesser business of the house.*" [1]

As she also had a large farm to run, it was clear to her that she also needed help with the work outside of the house. In July of 1823, she bought – for $550 – her first enslaved person, Frank Hawkins, who had been sold away from his wife and young son, Frank

*Quarters where enslaved persons lived still stand on the grounds of the Academy.*

Jr. Records indicate that there were several items bought for Frank, including a shirt, coat, blanket, tobacco, and shoes; the purchase of tools in 1837 for $10.81 suggests that he must have been a skilled carpenter. He later became a trusted, diligent worker who managed the work of the plantation and often went to Opelousas to make purchases of meat and supplies for the convent. For this he would have had to carry a pass to allow him to be on the road unaccompanied.[2] A copy of the bill of sale for Frank is found in the school's museum, as are other artifacts and documents telling the stories of the Academy's enslaved persons.

In addition to the *House Journal*, census and accounting records provide a glimpse into the business of slavery. Births, marriages, and deaths are found in the census records, while purchases of clothing, food, and shoes are listed in the convent accounts. Numerous payments – for items such as one dozen shoes ($5), clothing ($35.93), and a dozen women's head coverings ($4) – indicate that over the years the convent owned a considerable number of enslaved persons.

The growth of religion through catechesis, or instruction in Catholicism, among the Academy's enslaved persons is reflected in the many accounts of their Baptisms, First

*Enslaved persons who worked at the Academy in the 1800s are commemorated on a plaque outside the quarters where they resided.*

Communions, Confirmations, marriages and final sacraments before death. It is recorded that on June 26, 1829, "*Mélite, our negress*" [3] received the sacrament of Baptism with two of the pupils, and that on July 20 that same year, the school acquired Martin, the husband of Mélite. He received Baptism on August 15, 1829, and then "*was legitimately married in the Church.*" [4] The *House Journal* records the death of "*...Martin, [who] died rather suddenly from an absess [sic] which strangled him. He had been to confession only 15 days before. R.I.P.*" [5] Mélite, his widow, would live to be 101 years old, dying in 1859.

On the Feast of the Immaculate Conception, December 8, 1829, "*Jenny, wife of Frank, our negro, and her two children, Francis [Frank, Jr.] and Ben, have finally come to live here, full of gratitude to Mother Xavier, who brought them in order to alleviate their lot.*" [6] "*Mother Xavier has also purchased Julia and David (brother of Jenny), who were married at church the same day David came to us.*" [7]

In October of 1834, much construction on the plantation was taking place, some of it intended for the growing worker families. "*The walls of a new brick structure are being built, to house the kitchen,* dépense, *vestry, a room for ironing, and the laundry.*

**34**  *Academy of the Sacred Heart at Grand Coteau*

*It is also about this time that we are building a place for our three families of Negroes, also, another small structure in the garden to serve as a bakery."* [8] The three families are probably Martin and Melite, a couple in their 60s, Frank and Jenny (Hawkins) with three boys 10 and younger, and newly married David and Julia (Eaglin). [9]

The workers' living quarters were expanded to accommodate growing families in the 1850s.

In less than 20 years, the population at the Academy had grown significantly. At that time, in the 1840s, living on the grounds were 100 students, 20 Religious, and 20 enslaved persons, ten of whom can be identified as extended family members of Frank and Jenny Hawkins. The workload increased as well, including planting, cultivating, and harvesting more crops, maintaining a dairy and chicken coops, sewing and laundering clothing and bedding, carrying water from the wells, cleaning the buildings, building fences, and providing transport. All these required the skills and labor of the workers, many of whom learned new and marketable trades, in order to ensure continuous operation of the Academy.

\* \* \* \* \*

At this time in Louisiana, riots were breaking out in various parts of the state. The following is a September 1, 1840, article from the *New Orleans Picayune* and reprinted in *The Liberator*, an anti-slavery newspaper.

*A Negro revolt. Abolition incendiaries are creeping among us like moles in the ground, as blind, as difficult to catch, and as mischievous. Four hundred happy and peaceful slaves having been wrought upon by some of those sneaking pests to our well-being, broke out in furious revolt on the 25th... in the Parish of Lafayette; but the poor misguided blacks were soon taught their error, and forty of them were placed in confinement, while twenty were sentenced to be hung upon the 27th. Four white abolition rascals were detected, acting as leaders in conjunction with one yellow fellow, who is notorious for being a great scoundrel. It is the white incendiaries that ought to be hung, or, if the poor misled slaves must suffer, double, treble, should be the punishment imposed upon those heartless emissaries of a fanatical and reckless sect.* [10]

Much drama consumed the Lafayette community on that first day in September of 1840. Caught in the net of suspects, Frank Hawkins and Ignatius Gough, an enslaved person of the Jesuits, were arrested. Gough was imprisoned for eight days and was reportedly tortured. When he was declared innocent after being defended by a Jesuit priest, Gough was able to return to his family. For an expense of $4 for transport, Hawkins, however, had been able to return the same day he had been held, as recounted in the following account from the *House Journal*:

*A plot of the negroes against the whites has caused at this time many court summons. Our poor Frank has been arrested: his family are plunged into grief. Jenny, his wife, goes sobbing to the feet of the Blessed Virgin, and all our good blacks pray to this Consoler of the Afflicted; the same evening Frank, declared innocent, came back to us. Our joy is great, and they all return to the chapel together to offer to God and to Mary their heart-felt gratitude.* [11]

A year and a half later, on February 9, 1842, the *House Journal* records the death of this much-beloved person.

*At 10:00 P.M. Frank, the oldest negro on the place, gave back his soul to his Creator, having received all the Sacraments some days before. A few moments before his death he asked his wife:* "Is Mass over yet?" *When she said it was, he replied:* "And I, also; I am finished; I am going to see Our Lord. Goodbye!" *He repeated this word many times, and died in perfect peace, recommending his soul to God. It was like a feast day for him, thinking that he was going to see again Mother Xavier Murphy [d. 9-6-1836], for whom he had always had a respect mingled with veneration.* [12]

Years later, in 1893, Frank's sister-in-law, "Aunt Julia" would die at the convent where she had lived since her arrival in 1834. Frank Hawkins was buried, as were all local enslaved persons, in the St. Charles Borromeo cemetery in the town of Grand Coteau. Almost all of Frank's descendants are buried there.

*Eliza Nebbitt was among the enslaved persons who served the needs of the Sacred Heart nuns, particularly Mother Hardey and Mother Audé during the foundation of St. Michael's school and convent.*

\* \* \* \* \*

The participation of the community as a whole spread to events not just tragic or prayerful, but also to amusement and fun. On January 13, 1841, there was "*... a grand congé for the community and the school – even for our workmen and our negroes. There was nothing but joy and happiness throughout the whole house.*" [13]

A celebration of the end of the school year in August of 1852 was particularly inventive and inclusive. "*Mother Praz had sent over a superb magic lantern; that evening everyone gathered in the 2nd* cours*, and the negroes assembled near the parlor, so that they, too, were able to enjoy the pictures, which lasted until 10:00 P.M.* "Hyacintha," *shown on the screen, delighted and interested everyone; they were consoled at not seeing all of it by our Mother's promise that the lantern would appear again sometime before vacation, if they were very good.*" [14]

In the 1850s eighteen enslaved persons lived at the Academy, and more cabins were built to house them. Purchases of eggs, chickens, hogs, clothing, and shoes as well as payment for work on Sundays are noted in the convent accounts. By 1860, a considerable number – two-thirds – of the Academy's enslaved persons had been born there and were members of the extended family of Frank and Jenny Hawkins, and her brother David and his wife. The final sales and purchases of slaves for the Academy happened between 1858 and 1860, with no purchases occurring after the Civil War began. [15]

# Chapter 6

# Civil War and the Academy

The four decades between the founding of the school and the worst destruction of the Civil War saw substantial growth of the Academy. During this time, new building construction, new pupils, new teachers, and new members of the Religious of the Sacred Heart all contributed to the work to fulfill the mission of Madeleine Sophie Barat and Philippine Duchesne.

The Academy's reputation for good schooling and a healthful environment in a time of area-wide illness spread so that by 1834 the enrollment reached the 100 mark. The Religious had to turn away students until they could provide room for more.

With the coming of the Jesuits to the area, retreats began to be offered for the students and the Religious. In 1853, the first retreat for Ladies of the World was given. Days of Reflection for lay women were introduced later and would become a highly valued tradition, often experienced in the season of Lent.

In addition to recording the school's growth during antebellum times, the *House Journal* chronicles the many deaths in the Community, often as a result of fever and sometimes cholera. A poignant passage in the *Journal* on August 31, 1843, describes a particularly memorable death:

*"Our Lord called to Himself Sr. Josephine Déjean after a year of continued suffering. She constantly edified us, in health as well as in sickness, by her exactitude to the Rule and her perfect obedience – no one ever saw her fail in the slightest degree. When we asked her what gave a religious soul the greatest consolation at the moment of death, 'Fidelity to the Rule,' she replied. She gave proof of her obedience up to her last breath.*

*"The infirmarian, leaving her at two hours after midnight, said to her, 'Now, Sr.* Déjean, do not go and die during my absence!' *She replied,* 'I am not able, Mother, to keep myself from dying tonight.' *The Superior, having entered the infirmary at five the next morning, this dear Sister, although in her agony, tried to smile at her as if to say,* 'I've been waiting for you!' *Although she could not speak, she remained conscious until her last breath; she died that morning immediately after receiving a final absolution. She was buried that same evening because of the intense heat."* [1]

\* \* \* \* \*

The Annual Letters giving the RSCJ motherhouse in Paris an accounting of each year's progress at Grand Coteau, St. Michael's, and Natchitoches had been prevented by the Civil War. Therefore, in July of 1864, Reverend Mother Amélie Jouve, the superior vicar and a niece of Philippine Duchesne, supplied notes covering events of 1859 to

1864. Additionally, Louise Callan's definitive history, *The Society of the Sacred Heart in North America*, published in 1937, provides a vivid account of the Society's operations in Louisiana during the War Between the States.

In the early weeks of 1861, Louisiana was caught up in the secession movement that swept from South Carolina to Texas, and on January 26 Louisiana seceded from the Union. The Religious of the Sacred Heart of Louisiana, who *"were Southerners by birth or sympathy,"* [2] had heard much discussion of the economic and political situation facing the nation. They knew they would be confronted with the prospect of war. However, during the early months of the impending storm *"life ran smoothly enough."* [3]

While the position of St. Michael's on the Mississippi River exposed that community to greater danger, the isolation of Grand Coteau sheltered it from much of the destruction, so much so that many New Orleans families fled the city after it fell to the Union and took refuge in the Opelousas area, near Grand Coteau. As a consequence, the Academy experienced a sudden increase in enrollment, filling the school with 80 boarders and 50 day students.

The annalist for the Society wrote in her *Lettres Annuelles 1863-1866* that the pupils adapted to their new circumstances and began doing various forms of manual labor, particularly household chores.

*"Divided into bands, with a religious at the head of each, they learned all kinds of manual and household work, taking turns in the care of the dormitories, the refectory, the kitchen, at the dishwashing and the ironing. Some even asked to learn all that concerned the dairy. And these occupations filled, not the class periods, but the time formerly given to piano lessons, practice of music and art."* [4]

As the conflict intensified, conditions worsened and the nuns were uncertain how they would continue to feed the children now in their care as resources were diminishing daily. An answer to their many prayers came through a most unexpected channel: a Yankee general.

Union General Nathaniel Banks had succeeded General Benjamin Butler in December of 1862 as the Commander of the Department of the Gulf. Turning his attention away from New Orleans to southwestern Louisiana, Banks took on the 3,000 Confederate soldiers of General Richard Taylor, pouring into the Teche country. It was a spirited campaign from Lafourche to Opelousas and it put Banks in Grand Coteau.

On an April morning in 1863, Mother Jouve received an unanticipated but most welcome letter from Gen. Banks in which he alluded to the fact that his daughter was a pupil at a Sacred Heart school in New York. Aware that his campaign would take him near the Grand Coteau area, Gen. Banks' wife had implored him to offer his protection to the nuns and students at the Academy. The following and subsequent letters fulfilled his wife's wishes: [5]

**38** *Academy of the Sacred Heart at Grand Coteau*

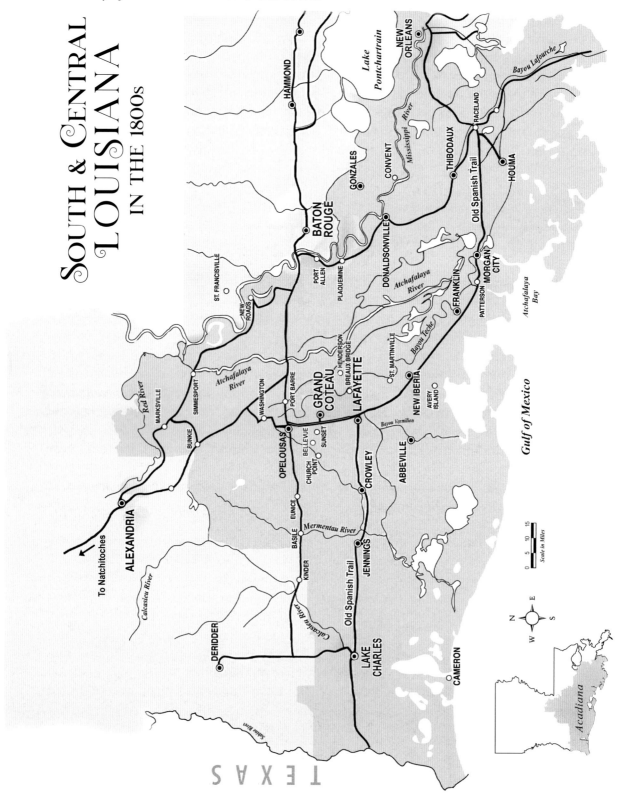

*Civil War and the Academy* **39**

*Headquarters, Army of the Gulf,*
*Grand Coteau, Apr. 20, 1863. 8 A.M.*
*To the Superior of the Convent of the Sacred Heart:*
*"If you desire to send letters to New York, you will please forward them to me by the bearer, who is instructed to wait for them. I send a safeguard that will protect your school from the struggles in the rear of my column, and if you desire it will leave a guard. I regret that I cannot call to see you. My daughter is with Madame [Mother Aloysia] Hardey at New York. Mrs. Banks, who visited the school but a short time since, writes that all are well there.*

*I am respectfully*
*Yr Obt Servant*
*N.P. Banks*
*M.G.C.*

One can but imagine Mother Jouve's surprise and joy at receiving such an assurance.

General Banks' offer to help was answered prayer. A few days later, Mother Jouve received the following letter: [6]

*To the Lady Superior,*
*Convent at Grand Coteau.*
*Dear Madame,*
*Accept my thanks for your note. The favor to which it refers is too slight for reference. I have ordered the Commissary in Chief to forward to your Order at the Convent small quantities of flour, coffee, tea, fine salt, and other articles that may be useful – which I beg you will accept – if you get them – with my regards.*

*Army movements are uncertain. If you have any requests to make, desire to go or send to New Orleans, inform me soon.*

*It grieves me that I cannot see you and your Sisters. I think we should be friends, as with your leave I subscribe myself,*

*Yours truly, N.P. Banks, M.G.C.*

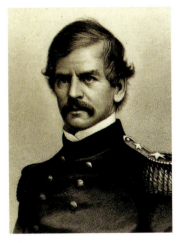

*Union Gen. Nathaniel Banks sent letters to Mother Amélie Jouve, superior of the Academy at the time of the Civil War, promising to protect and provide for the school and those associated with it. Fortuitously, Gen. Banks had a daughter who attended another Sacred Heart School, in New York. His wife had urged him to assure the safety of the Grand Coteau nuns and those under their protection – a request to which he acceded.*

**40**  *Academy of the Sacred Heart at Grand Coteau*

The General was true to his promise, and on April 29 Mother Jouve took receipt of 100 pounds of coffee, 2 barrels of flour, 1 barrel of sugar, 5 barrels of meal, one-half chest of tea and 5 bags of salt. These were accompanied by the General's *"personal regard for...those connected with the institution...."* [7] Soon a bolt of black merino wool and a keg of butter came to the convent. More importantly, Banks sent troops to protect and ensure the safety of the nuns and students: [8]

*Headquarters, 4 May, 1863*
*Officers and Soldiers will protect the property and persons of the Convent and College of Grand Coteau. The violation of this safeguard will be punished with death.*

*N. P. Banks, M.G.C.*

In his last known letter to Mother Jouve, Banks expressed his great pleasure in complying with her requests and asked for her prayers. But he wasn't finished yet. In August, he had further provisions sent to the convent and assured the nuns that he would supply whatever was needed in the way of clothing and food. He provided the transport of letters to Mother Aloysia Hardey, RSCJ, in New York. He also wrote a letter of safe conduct for Mother Shannon from St. Michael's to Grand Coteau, as well as one of free passage of a convoy of provisions through Federal lines between the convents at Grand Coteau and Natchitoches.

Because of answered prayers and the intervention of General Banks, the Academy suffered no material damage from the fighting in the area in 1863. The crops from their farm and orchard were respected, so fruit and crops could be gathered for preserving. The community was even able to make altar wine from the abundant wild grape vines growing in the woods. However, a lot of the cattle had been "requisitioned."

But 1864 brought new and severe trials to the nuns at Grand Coteau. Communication between the Southern and Northern Sacred Heart schools was fraught with nearly insurmountable difficulties, a privation keenly felt by all. After Mother Jouve was sent to Paris to attend the General Council in early April, the nuns found her departure and the lack of further communication painful. Six months of uncertainty followed. Still counting on Mother Jouve's return, on November 1, Mother Martinez received word that Mother Jouve would not return and was to be replaced.

Fortunately, her replacement was Mother Anna Josephine Shannon, well known and appreciated by all in the community. It took nearly the whole of November for Mother Shannon to finally arrive as the blockades on all sides limited travel.

Almost as soon as she arrived, Mother Shannon learned that provisions she had bought and paid exorbitantly for had been confiscated by the Confederate government. This forced her to leave Coteau the day after her arrival. Determined to obtain justice on this matter, she traveled as far as Marshall, Texas, to bring the Academy's cause to court in a form of "*procés.*" [9] Confident that the court's decision would go her way, Mother Shannon returned to Coteau for several weeks. But the nuns soon learned that the court had decided against them.

To add insult to injury, the military would soon send an officer to seize the merchandise left at the convent. It was to be sold at a profit for the Confederate government. Desolation was great, for the nuns were on the verge of lacking everything necessary and of sending their pupils back to their parents. The nuns placed all their confidence in the Sacred Heart of Jesus and the intercession of St. Joseph. Novenas succeeded one another, and sacrifices were made which "*so changed the hearts of our enemies that all was arranged to our satisfaction.*" [10]

With the surrender of General Robert E. Lee to General Ulysses S. Grant on April 9, 1865, at Appomattox Court House, the hostilities between the Union and the Confederacy came to an end. For the nuns at Grand Coteau, the cessation of war allowed for much-needed correspondence with their sisters in the North and in Europe to begin again. But it also left a South devastated by war and residual hatred and revenge. While the property was not destroyed, the school's revenues were gone. Steps toward recovery had to be taken.

At this same time, the Religious of the Sacred Heart learned of the death of their foundress, Mother Madeleine Sophie Barat, on May 25, 1865. On that previous Sunday, she had told her Community, "*I was very anxious to see you today, for on Thursday we are going to heaven.*" [11] Stricken with cerebral congestion depriving her of speech, she received the last rites of the Church from a Jesuit priest and the blessing of Pope Pius IX transmitted to her by Msgr. De Mérode the day before she died. For 59 years, she had served as Superior General.

Now, with the confirmation of Mother Vicars from three continents, Mother Josephine Goetz was unanimously elected as the second Superior General of the Society.

The years following the surrender of Gen. Lee and the death of Mother Barat saw the Academy in Grand Coteau resuming the normal life of school and Community. While enrollment was reflective of the reduced circumstances of the families, new works expanding the mission to serve God's people were inaugurated. The Children of Mary gathered a group of former pupils and their friends each month for the Sodality meeting and sewing for poor churches. These women carried their enthusiasm into their parishes, serving as organists, sacristans, catechists and nurses to the poor. Annual retreats increased and outreach into the mission fields expanded. Several new postulants arrived at the convent and many novices took the habit.

Chapter 7

# The Miracle of Grand Coteau

The miracle that occurred through the intercession of Blessed John Berchmans (pronounced berkmanz) in December of 1866 remains the most remarkable spiritual event in the Academy's history. The *House Journal* records this supernatural phenomenon:

*"December 14 – Miraculous cure of a young postulant, Miss Mary Wilson, obtained by a novena made to Bl. John Berchmans."* [1]

Mary Wilson herself provided a detailed account of the events related to the miracle. Quoted here are excerpts from her testimony, titled *Sr. Mary Wilson's Attestation Concerning Her Miraculous Cure through the Intercession of St. John Berchmans.* (sic: He was not canonized until 1888.) A fuller account of her life, including her miraculous cure, can be found on pages 124-125.

*"I left St. Louis on the 18th of June, 1866, to enter the Convent of the Sacred Heart at St. Michael's. I arrived...with a pain in my side, loss of appetite, general debility and great disgust for water.... The physician of the house said it was useless to try any other remedy, seeing that all he had done aggravated my sufferings instead of relieving them.... Mother Superior (Martinez) had the kindness to send me to Grand Coteau, thinking that by change of air I would recover my health....*

*"On the 19th of October, I was obliged to repair to the Infirmary and I did not leave it until the 15th of December, the day after the one on which God was pleased to manifest His Power and Mercy on my behalf."*

Being desperately ill and begging God for intervention, Mary prayed for a miracle.

*"Then placing the image of Bld. Berchmans on my mouth, I said 'If it be true that you can work miracles, I wish you would do something for me; if not, I will not believe in you....'"*

Her prayer was answered. John Berchmans appeared to her and she was healed through his intercession.

*"I sat up in bed, I felt no pain, I was afraid it was an illusion and that my cure was not real. I turned over and over in my bed, without pain.*

**Mary Wilson**

*I then exclaimed, 'It is true, Bld. Berchmans has cured me.' ... In about three-quarters of an hour Mother Superior (Rev. Mother Martinez) came in to see me, fearing at the same time to find me in the agonies of death, but what was her great surprise when she met my eyes and heard me wish her 'Good morning.' ...I told her that I was cured and had recovered the use of my eyes and tongue and craved permission to get up. Mother then approached me and kissed me."*

Mary's testimony goes on to recount the measures taken by Mother Martinez to ensure that she had been cured, including refusing her permission to get out of bed. When Mary did finally get up to have the bedding changed, a witness reported that Mary danced with a chair around the infirmary. The next morning, Mary enjoyed a hearty breakfast of chicken, toast, and coffee and later enjoyed a noon dinner.

Her Community congratulated her and marveled at the goodness of God and the intercession of Blessed John Berchmans.

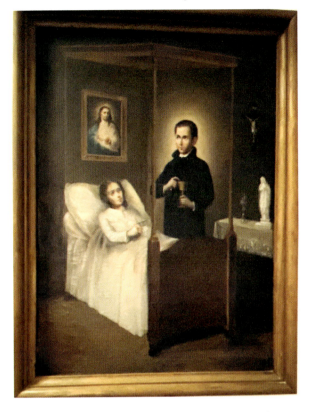

*The miraculous cure of Mary Wilson through the intercession of Blessed John Berchmans occurred on December 14, 1866, at the Academy of the Sacred Heart in Grand Coteau.*

When Doctor Millard visited her that evening, he was surprised when Mary answered the door for him. After hearing her story and questioning her about her activities, he expressed his surprise and declared that "no human means could ever have produced such an effect." [2]

The following Monday, December 17, Mary reported:

*"...my dearest hopes were accomplished. I received the Holy Habit of the Order of the Sacred Heart from the hands of Reverend Father Benausse and in the presence of a number of people who, hearing of my miraculous cure, were anxious to be present at the ceremony of my being clad in the religious garb...."*

*"I hereby declare, under the sanctity of my oath, that the above statement, according to the best of my knowledge and belief, is entirely true."* (Signed by Mary Wilson, Novice of the Sacred Heart at Grand Coteau, February 15, 1867.)

Fr. M. Nachon, S.J., wrote to Mary indicating that a formal inquiry would be made and that there were many people who could testify under oath to the truth of what they

*The Shrine of St. John Berchmans is located in the room where the miracle occurred.*

witnessed. He told Mary:

"*You see, child, that the time of miracles is not entirely passed away. There is nothing astonishing for us Catholics, since we know that nothing is impossible to God.*"[3]

Mary Wilson's cure was the third and final miracle needed for the canonization of Blessed John Berchmans.

A document verifying that this miracle occurred on December 14, 1866, is displayed in the Academy's former infirmary, which has been converted into the Shrine of St. John Berchmans.

One visitor to the Shrine in the late 1880s was transformed by her visit. Her story, recounted in the *Lettres Annuelles 1886-1887*, follows in translation:

"*The little sanctuary dedicated to Bld. Berchmans became a center of attraction; ... Jesuits... request the favor of celebrating the Blessed Sacrament [Holy Sacrifice] of Mass in the very place where the apparitions took place. Our dear children also have the privilege of attending there sometimes, and the numerous petitions that they send to the young saint witness to their faith and their trust.*

"*The people of the world come there to visit it/him with veneration and to obtain some worthy graces.... Allow us to cite one. Mme X, belonging to Protestantism, lived in a city in Texas which unfortunately did not have one Catholic. For some time, however, she began to have doubts, and looked to self-instruction by reading books of controversy. The questionable points were then submitted to her brother, a devout Catholic, residing in California; this one would spare nothing to illuminate this soul so right, avid to knowing the truth.*

"*The light entered little by little, but a shadow still remained: the worship of the Saints, the miracles, the apparitions in particular could not be accepted. One day, she caught sight of by accident, in a public paper, the relationship of the apparitions of the Bld. Berchmans, followed by the miraculous healing of our dear Sister Wilson.*

"*Her resolution was immediately made to go to the location of the apparitions. The Priest, who had finished instructing her and finding her sufficiently ready, administered the Sacraments of Baptism and Eucharist to her before her travel. Then the newly converted headed towards Coteau, where, in a few words, she declared the goal of her visit.*

"*One of ours took her then to the pious sanctuary. 'Let us kneel,' she (religious) says, and let us make a prayer together to the Beatified. 'Yes,' responds Mme. X, 'ask faith for me.' After a few invocations, followed by a moment of silence, the newly converted stood up ... flooded with tears, all her doubts had disappeared at the feet of the Beatified. She could not contain the surges of her happiness.*

"*She left us full of gratitude, and a few days later our honorable Mother received a letter where she was thankful again for the welcome so cordial that she had found at S.C. [Sacred Heart] that she rightly named: 'Paradise on earth.*'"[4]

The Academy of the Sacred Heart has the only shrine in the United States situated in the exact location where a miracle has taken place. Visitors from around the world, as well as Academy faculty and staff, continue to visit and pray in the Shrine, sometimes leaving intentions and prayer requests. Students at the Academy can often be found in the Shrine, stopping in for quiet contemplation and a quick prayer, especially before an exam.

*Mary Wilson is buried in the Academy's cemetery. The original marker on her grave (far left) was replaced by a newer one in 2008.*

# Chapter 8

# Educating a Newly Freed People

When the winds of the Civil War blew into the quiet, little town of Grand Coteau, the nuns anticipated the emancipation of enslaved persons, and in 1862 they took steps to do just that.

*...Our house was almost the only establishment which was still open; families the most respectable confided their children to us, hoping, as we did, that our solitude would remain impenetrable to the armies. However, foreseeing the future, we believed it our duty to instruct our children and initiate them into the new situation which Providence was preparing for them, by advising them to free their slaves.* [1]

After the surrender at Appomattox and the cessation of war, the Religious of the Sacred Heart in Grand Coteau and other parts of Louisiana were faced with a South nearly destroyed by the war. Planters had no money to send their daughters to the Academy, since so many plantations were devastated. Families were indigent, resources were depleted, and the social fabric was virtually destroyed. While the Academy buildings survived the war without destruction, the revenues generated were gone. *"Only the fidelity of the Negroes on the plantations made possible a partial recovery."* [2]

In May of 1865, the workers at Grand Coteau were assembled by Mother Martinez to hear an offer made through the convent property overseer, Benjamin Smith:

*The Negroes were free; they could take advantage of their liberty, leave the plantation and seek employment elsewhere, or they could remain in the brick quarters which had sheltered them since the days of Mother Xavier Murphy, continue to work as they had done hitherto and receive from the nuns food and clothing and the attentive care of religious charity. There could be no question of regular wages yet, for money was as scarce at the convent as on any other Southern estate, but they were sure of fair treatment and had the prospect of bettering themselves, as times and conditions improved.* [3]

It is noteworthy that seven families of those newly emancipated chose to stay with the Religious at ASH. It was a familiar and safe place where they had reared their children and established roots. Had they not remained, the Academy would have been in even more dire straits.

Some of their descendants, particularly those of Frank and Jenny Hawkins, still live in the Grand Coteau area, while many others have moved to various parts of the United States, from California to the East Coast.

\* \* \* \* \*

In the wake of the Civil War, the need for education for the newly freed people was recognized by the Second Plenary Council of Baltimore and Louisiana Archbishop Odin, whose goal was to evangelize the former slaves and to teach them how to use *"the liberty they had so lately acquired."* [4]

The Archbishop felt that the cooperation of religious orders of women was a necessity. Realizing that the undertaking would face many difficulties, he chose Reverend Mother Anna Shannon, RSCJ, who was known for her tact, prudence, and intrepidity – qualities much needed for this new enterprise.

Mother Shannon eloquently pleaded the cause of the freed children in *"a truly Catholic spirit,"* as can be seen in her letter to Reverend Mother Josephine Goetz:

*"Archbishop Odin has broached the delicate question of undertaking the education of the Negroes. So far, not a single Community has accepted the work. They all fear that in so doing they will harm their academies. He begs me to tell you that our Holy Father has recommended to him the care and salvation of these poor black people, and he urges us to take up the work of teaching little Negro girls in the parish here, promising that he will not insist on a continuation of the work, if it proves in any way detrimental to the convent.*

*"... Many of our Louisiana Negroes are Catholics, in name at least, and we long to save the souls of these poor people. The Archbishop says his plea will be greatly strengthened if we step forward and give the example. There is a building on our property some distance from the convent, entirely separated from both the boarding school and the free day school, which would serve the purpose of a school for the Negroes. If you approve, my very Reverend Mother, I will make the attempt.*

*"While awaiting your answer in this matter, I am going to sound the dispositions of several influential people. I have already spoken to Reverend Father Bellanger, Superior of the Marists. He says he cannot open a Negro school yet without damaging his college, but he thinks it is quite different with us, just because of our prestige, and that no one in Louisiana could take the initiative better than I."* [5]

Mother Shannon's efforts and commitment led to the establishment of a free school in Convent, Louisiana, to educate the children of formerly enslaved persons there. Soon after, the religious at Grand Coteau would follow her lead. On May 3, 1875, the nuns in Grand Coteau opened a school on the Academy grounds beginning with 16 female students for the express purpose of educating the children of the workers on a broader academic level.

The *House Journal* notes this new establishment:

*"Today we opened a school for our little negresses. Some time ago a negro in the village had opened a school, and the number of his pupils rose to 60. Although he was not a Catholic, he made no objection to the Jesuit Fathers coming to give instructions from time to time. Fr. Olivier, superior at the College and so zealous for the glory of God, spoke to Rev. Mother of his desire for us to open a school for the negroes here, so that these poor children might have the opportunity of getting a Christian education. Today, the first day of classes, 16 children came to the Convent."* [6]

Classes were held first in a room in the laundry until the school – called the Colored School of the Sacred Heart – could be built, in 1888-89, about a mile from the Academy. The need for more room was apparent. With contributions from the Archbishop of New

**48** *Academy of the Sacred Heart at Grand Coteau*

Orleans, the Superior General of the Society of the Sacred Heart, and the Jesuits of St. Charles College, a new building was erected on the convent grounds, eventually including both boys and girls. There were difficulties facing the new enterprise: the students often needed to work in the fields during planting and harvesting seasons, there were distances to be covered to get to school, and other challenges to be faced. But the school prospered, and by 1890 there were 150 male and female students enrolled. By 1939, the school was moved into the Grand Coteau corporate limits and was named Saint Peter Claver School. Margaret Mary Finn, RSCJ, served as the school's principal from 1941 to 1947. Enrollment remained high, as did Catholic vocations, especially into the Order of the Holy Family. By 1946, there were nearly 300 boys and girls in grades 1 to 10.

They were taught practical skills, such as home economics and carpentry, as well as religion and literacy. Religious vocations matured as 25 young women became Sisters of the Holy Family and one young man became a priest and another a brother by 1947. The 1946-47 school year was the last that the Religious of the Sacred Heart were in charge. The graduation celebration included the pastor, the renowned Fr. Cornelius Thensted, S.J.

The next school year, the Sisters of the Holy Family took over the operation of St. Peter Claver. However, the Religious of the Sacred Heart continued to teach in the high school until the 1960s. St. Peter Claver High School would close in 1977 and the building would be renovated later for use as the Thensted Center.

By 1982, under the direction of Sr. Margaret "Mike" Hoffman, the Religious of the Sacred Heart established the Thensted Center as a mission to help the financially disadvantaged of the area. The Outreach Center, supported by St. Charles Borromeo Parish, plus donations, grants and government funding sources, provides essentials like food and clothing, home visits to the shut-ins, and a thrift store. Additionally, the Center provides tutoring, often by the older students from the Academy, summer enrichment programs, counseling services, education for senior citizens, emergency transportation, a health clinic, a sub-bank, and rooms for community events such as weddings, town meetings, and retreats.

Another school that was started by the RSCJ in Grand Coteau, opening on Easter Monday, April 7, 1890, was called Sacred Heart Parochial School. It is now known as St. Ignatius Elementary School and includes grades Pre-K through 8. The nuns administered the school until 1950 and then resumed running it from 1975 to 1986. A Diocese of Lafayette school, St. Ignatius continues under the leadership of laity.

\* \* \* \* \*

The impact of the inspiration and work of the Society of the Sacred Heart still resonates throughout the Grand Coteau community. On February 25, 2001, the community of St. Charles Borromeo Parish commended the Religious of the Sacred Heart for their continuing social outreach and ministry to the needs of others and proclaimed that they are a significant part of Black history in Grand Coteau.

*Educating a Newly Freed People* **49**

*Answering the need for educational opportunities for the children of newly freed people of the Academy and Grand Coteau, the Religious of the Sacred Heart started a school for girls. Opened in 1875, it was called the Colored School of the Sacred Heart. Eventually the enterprise moved into Grand Coteau and included boys, and in 1939 it became known as St. Peter Claver School.*
**Above:** *In 1952, Sisters from both the Society of the Sacred Heart (RSCJ) and Sisters of the Holy Family (SSF) posed with their pupils. From left to right are Mother Alphonsus, SSF; Mother Marguerite Baudelle, RSCJ; and Mother Sebastian, SSF.* **Below:** *In 1922, male pupils posed with their teacher (top row at right).*

*Fr. Cornelius Thensted, S.J., worked tirelessly in Grand Coteau and nearby Bellevue for more than 25 years to teach and shepherd the descendants of slaves. Sr. Margaret "Mike" Hoffman, RSCJ, founded the Thensted Center to continue Fr. Thensted's work of assisting the Black community of the area.*

The citation reads:
*Blessed are they who serve the Lord.*
*Our community of faith honors the Religious of the Sacred Heart for ministering to others' needs, for cheering hearts with thoughtful deeds, for walking closely in His way, for dedicating each new day to humble service, doing good, and teaching love and brotherhood. May he reward you with His love and countless blessings from above.*
*We give you our love and our prayers. You are a part of our Black History here in St. Charles Parish.*

\* \* \* \* \*

In 2018, when the Society of the Sacred Heart celebrated 200 years of the presence of the Religious of the Sacred Heart in the United States, it also committed itself to an exploration of the Society's participation in the culture of slavery and to a better understanding of the pervasive issue of racism. The Committee on Slavery, Accountability and Reconciliation, formed by the RSCJ Provincial in 2016, was mandated to uncover people's stories, to honor their memories, and to begin to heal relationships.

Many of those stories come from Grand Coteau and find their roots in the early years of the Academy's existence, when enslaved persons were an integral part of the school's life. Essential to reconciliation is the recognition, acknowledgement, and appreciation of the fact that the work of enslaved persons at Grand Coteau was vital to the everyday operations at the school. Using the bricks which they made, they helped to build the main structures, some of which still stand today. They worked with the sisters to take care of the students, assisting with meals, sewing, mending clothing, doing laundry, and maintaining the gardens that not only provided various vegetables and fruits such as peaches and figs, but also beauty. They farmed and cared for the animals. They dug the graves and acted as pall bearers. They helped to keep the whole institution running.

*A monument, located in the Grand Coteau community cemetery, commemorates the enslaved persons who worked at the Academy and who are buried here.*

In September of 2018, the Academy hosted a gathering of descendants of enslaved persons and various members of the Society and the school community, at which the creation of a scholarship fund for African-American students to attend the Academy and the Berchmans school was announced. Called the *Cor Unum* Scholarship, it also provides professional development for faculty and staff and course curriculum on inclusion and diversity.

As a highlight of the event, the group dedicated a monument in the parish cemetery which names the convent's enslaved persons who are buried there. Additionally, the school's museum features a room that recounts various stories, displays photographs, and lists the names of all known enslaved persons who had worked at the Academy. A plaque naming those living there in its first years was placed at the former slave quarters. The Academy made additional plans for other future gatherings to commemorate the enslaved men and women who once lived and worked at the school.

The Academy of the Sacred Heart at Grand Coteau, in partnership with the Network of Sacred Heart Schools, is committed to eliminating racism. While lifting up through its mission of education many generations of people – including children of former enslaved persons – the Academy acknowledges that it also owned human beings; therefore, the school has implemented a curriculum that addresses the part of its history that involves slavery. Teaching that history while being active agents of change honors the inherent, God-given dignity of all.

The Goals and Criteria clearly express the Academy's sincere intentions: "The school, drawing from Catholic Social Teaching, educates students to analyze and work to eradicate social structures, practices, systems, and values that perpetuate racism and other injustices."

# Chapter 9

# *Mater Admirabilis!*
(Mother Most Admirable!)

In the mid-1800s, when the Academy in Grand Coteau was just a couple decades into its mission, a young French Sacred Heart postulant was sitting down to paint an image of the Blessed Mother that would become known around the world.

The artist was Pauline Perdrau, and she titled her painting *Madonna of the Lily*. The iconic image would soon become known as *Mater Admirabilis*, and today it can be found in every Sacred Heart school in the world, whether in the form of a painting, a statue or even etched glass.

The story begins in Rome's *Trinità dei Monti* in 1844, several years after the founding of the Society. In 1828, the Religious of the Sacred Heart took over the maintenance and occupancy of the building at the top of the Spanish Steps. It was originally founded as a monastery during the fifteenth century, but because it was going to be abandoned, Pope Leo XII offered it to the Society of the Sacred Heart.

Opening a convent and a school there, the Society occupied it for more than 175 years, until September 1, 2006, when the Society withdrew from the building. The Community of Emmanuel now operates it and offers free access to *Mater*. Visitors from around the world, many of whom are alumnae and their families, visit to see *Mater Admirabilis*.

The artistically talented Pauline Perdrau begged permission of the Reverend Mother Josephine de Coriolis to paint an image of Our Lady in the corridor that led to the cloister. Reverend Mother was hesitant. Although she recognized Pauline's talent, she also knew of her inexperience with fresco painting techniques. After much prayer, she finally gave Pauline permission to make an attempt at the portrait. Pauline started work on June 1, 1844, working six to seven hours a day.

When the painting was completed, on July 1, the wet fresco colors were too vivid and garish for Mother Superior's taste, so the painting was concealed by a curtain for several weeks while the paint dried. The first people to actually view the painting were the community and the school's Children of Mary, who visited on the day the fresco was unveiled.

Contrary to the anecdote that Pope Pius IX named the painting, it was actually Mother Makrina, Abbess of the Basilian Nuns of Minsk, who suggested the title *Mater Admirabilis*, when she was staying at the *Trinità* for an extended visit. On October 20, 1846, Pope Pius IX visited *Trinità dei Monti* to bless the painting under its now-familiar name, *Mater Admirabilis*, Mother Most Admirable.

The painting portrays a young Mary, clothed in a rose-colored gown, before she became the mother of Jesus. At her side is a lily to symbolize her purity, near her are a distaff and spindle symbolizing her love of work, and at her feet is a book illustrating her

*Mater Admirabilis* **53**

*Original oil painting of* Mater Admirabilis *by Pauline Perdrau, dated 1867, is on display in the Academy in Grand Coteau. It was acquired sometime between 1903 and 1907 from a Sacred Heart house in France.*

### A Prayer to *Mater*

*Mater Admirabilis*, Mother Most Admirable of our Lord Jesus Christ, we know you as a woman of great faith and devotion, who gives patiently of herself to others. This service is embodied in the basket and spindle at your side. The book signifies an awareness of the value of knowledge and wisdom, and the lily is symbolic of your pureness. Your being reflects peace and contemplation and gentleness. All of these things make you, *Mater*, a model of womanhood for all of us. Teach us to grow in awareness of the uniqueness of womanhood and to who God asks us to be. We honor you with a crown of our rings, and ask you to be with us in our celebration today of the Word and Presence of your Son and our Savior, Jesus Christ.

– *Jeanne Adele Pavy*, Class of 1983

## 54 *Academy of the Sacred Heart at Grand Coteau*

dedication to study.

The story of the fresco spread quickly, and miracles have been associated with it. For instance, in November of 1846, a missionary of the Congregation of the Holy Heart of Mary was given back the power to speak, something he had completely lost. Pilgrims come to pray for grace and to kneel at the feet of Mary. Even Mother Madeleine Sophie Barat prayed there. Pope Pius IX gave permission for Mass to be offered there, and from that approval has grown the celebration of *Mater* in every Sacred Heart school around the world with an annual Mass on or near October 20. At the Academy in Grand Coteau, a weekend close to that date has become the annual alumnae reunion weekend.

## About the Artist

Born April 20, 1815, **Pauline Perdrau** greatly impacted the Sacred Heart community when as a young French novice she asked Mother Josephine de Coriolis for permission to paint a fresco of Mary on the wall at the *Trinità dei Monti* in Rome, Italy. That painting, *Mater Admirabilis*, has become an iconic symbol of the Religious of the Sacred Heart.

While she is best known for her painting of *Mater*, Pauline was also a gifted writer who recorded her life with Mother Madeleine Sophie Barat and Mother Josephine Goetz in her memoir, *Les Loisirs de l'Abbeye*.

Pauline's mother, a lifelong friend of Madeleine Sophie's, had thought of becoming a religious; Sophie told her that her vocation was that of marriage and family. But her daughter Pauline did become a religious. Indeed, Pauline knew from an early age that she had a religious vocation. She also had artistic talent and began drawing everything around her. In 1839 she was commissioned to paint the official portrait of Archbishop de Quelen, who assured her that her vocation was to the Sacred Heart.

Pauline entered the Society of the Sacred Heart on April 9, 1844, and in June began painting *Madonna of the Lily*, as *Mater* was originally called, completing the fresco in July of 1844. The following year she left Rome, never to return, and lived in France for the rest of her life. She made her first vows on April 23, 1847, and her final profession on February 2, 1853.

Near the end of her life, at the request of her only brother, Joseph, a priest, Pauline painted another image of Mary; this one was of the older Mary. Joseph was writing a book about the life of the elderly Mary and he needed an image for the frontispiece of the book. His sister started the artwork during vacation in 1883 and finished it in September, calling it *Our Lady in the House of St. John.*

Pauline painted other images of *Mater Admirabilis*, and one of those original paintings from 1867 hangs in the Academy of the Sacred Heart in Grand Coteau.

Pauline Perdrau died in France on October 5, 1895.

– *A'Jani Wiley,* Class of 2023

**Pauline Perdrau, RSCJ**

# Chapter 10

# The 19th Century Comes to an End

The late 1860s and 1870s saw the Society of the Sacred Heart's growth not only in Grand Coteau but in other parts of the United States as more Sacred Heart schools were opened. Among them was a day school in New Orleans, first located on Dumaine Street near St. Louis Cathedral and eventually relocated to St. Charles Avenue.

"The Rosary," as it is called, was placed under the patronage of *Mater Admirabilis,* as were other new schools established by the Society. People in New Orleans who knew the work of the RSCJ were delighted to have a sister-school in their city. From there, five postulants went to the Novitiate at Grand Coteau in 1867-68.

It was around this time that the veneration of *Mater Admirabilis* began in New Orleans, in Grand Coteau and at Sacred Heart schools around the world. The first mention of *Mater* in Grand Coteau's *House Journal* is found in the entry of October 21, 1865. The account tells of the students' desire to return to school early so that they could honor *Mater*:

*"Our children, who were supposed to return on the 21st, chose to come back on the 19th, in order to place under the protection of* Mater Admirabilis *the school year which was about to begin."* [1]

In 1872, Mother Aloysia Hardey, an illustrious alumna of Grand Coteau, approved Vicar Mother Shannon's decision to complete the convent building according to the original plans drawn up by the late Mother Xavier. Work was soon begun on the foundation of the east wing, which would include a library, parlors, classrooms, and accommodations.

On July 10, after the foundation had been blessed by Fr. Vialleton, an iron box – a sort of time capsule – was buried *"in the right angle which gives on the garden."* [2] Contained in the box were medals, the names of all the RSCJ Community members, names of all the pupils, and a prospectus of the school.

Religious observances, feast days, sodalities, Masses, various prayers and devotions were and are today integral parts of the daily lives of both the religious Community and the students. The school operates not only as an educational institution but also as a place of worship. Feast days celebrated include the Feasts of the Purification, the Sacred Heart, the Visitation, St. John Berchmans, and *Mater Admirabilis.*

A noteworthy novena to the Immaculate Conception involving the students was begun in November of 1882. The *House Journal* describes it in interesting detail:

*At the feet of the statue of the Blessed Virgin the word "Immaculata" is written in large letters. Each day one of the letters is uncovered, and for that day the school has a practice beginning with that letter: 1st day I – Intention, 2nd day M – Modesty, 3rd day M – Mortification, 4th day A – Application, 5th day C – Charity, 6th day U – Union, 7th*

**56** *Academy of the Sacred Heart at Grand Coteau*

*Sacred Heart nuns dressed in traditional black and white habits that changed very little in the first century and a half of their community's time in Grand Coteau. However, that custom would change decidedly as a result of the Second Vatican Council.*

day L – Louanges *(praise)*, 8th day A – Amiability, 9th day T – Travail *(work)*, and 10th day A – Amour *(love)*.

The novena is made in the evening before the Angelus in the big chapel, singing the litany of the Blessed Virgin. Five Children of Mary are privileged to carry five banners, on each of which is inscribed "IMMACULATA." One by one they advance, each one followed by her band. If the entire band has been faithful to the practice for that day, the banner is displayed. If, however, anyone has failed, part of the banner is rolled around the pole. If the child at fault expiates her failure by a penance, she is not humiliated.[3]

In the waning years of the 19th century, the school had its ups and downs, experiencing both challenges and joys, according to the *House Journal*: violent storms, especially area floods and unexpected heavy snow; heat waves at Christmas; "magic lantern" shows; annual enrollments numbering no more than 35 and grave illnesses and deaths of both students and Religious. The community also witnessed the Society's establishing of new schools in Grand Coteau; an increase in annual retreats; the death of Pope Pius IX, followed by the election of Leo XIII; and the canonization of St. John Berchmans on January 15, 1888.

# Part II

# The 20th Century

(1900-1999)

## Prayer to the Sacred Heart

O most holy Heart of Jesus, fountain of every blessing,
I adore you, I love you and with a lively sorrow for my sins.
I offer you this poor heart of mine.
Make me humble, patient, pure, and wholly obedient to your will.
Grant, good Jesus, that I may live in you and for you.
Protect me in the midst of danger; comfort me in my afflictions;
give me health of body, assistance in my temporal needs,
your blessings on all that I do, and the grace of a holy death.
Within your heart I place my every care.
In every need let me come to you with humble trust saying,
Heart of Jesus, help me.
Amen.

# Chapter 11

# A New Century

The twentieth century was one of great change: automobiles, world wars, societal upheavals, innovations in technology, votes for women, assassinations, moon landings. Through it all, the Academy of the Sacred Heart, while affected by these changes, remained steadfast in its mission of educating young women.

And in 1921, it celebrated the first century of its existence!

The centenary was co-celebrated with the centennial of St. John the Evangelist Parish in nearby Lafayette. The parish had opened its church doors in December of 1821, two months after the Academy began instructing its students. An account written by Louise Callan, RSCJ, describes the festive event:

*At Grand Coteau, still deep in its solitude, but enjoying all the improvements that modern invention has brought to rural life, a coincidence of dates made possible a magnificent celebration. The cathedral parish of Lafayette was founded the same year as the convent, 1821. Bishop Jules B. Jeanmard, as solicitous about the success of the one as the other, arranged that the parish jubilee should take place on the day preceding that of Grand Coteau, thus enabling a great assemblage of prelates to participate in both.*

*The Opelousas district had never before witnessed such a gathering. Cross-bearer and acolytes, twenty-one (parish) priests and eighteen Jesuits, a Benedictine abbot, six Monsignori and five bishops preceding Bishop Jeanmard of Lafayette and Archbishop Shaw of New Orleans, passed in colorful procession down the cedar alley, across the garden and up the avenue of pines, where the majestic giants of the Louisiana forest, rising to a height of more than ninety feet, seemed to pillar the blue dome above.*

*Within the chapel, the marble altar needed no other ornament than its golden tabernacle and Gothic candlesticks, brought from France in 1852. There were present venerable ladies of four score and ten years, who had finished their formal education at Grand Coteau nearly three quarters of a century before. They and their alumnae sisters rejoiced in the words of Father E. Mattern, S.J., whose sermon included a masterly and sympathetic interpretation of the Society's educational system.* [1]

That educational system still endures as the Academy commemorates a second century of cultivating in students their intellectual abilities and interests, while preparing them to develop into women of power – the power to do good in the world. While embracing many changes in the past 200 years, the school has never forgotten the primary mission of Madeleine Sophie Barat: "*to mould minds and hearts and wills for citizenship in the kingdom of Christ, a kingdom of time and eternity.*" [2]

Six years after the centennial celebration, the Academy as well as the Mississippi and

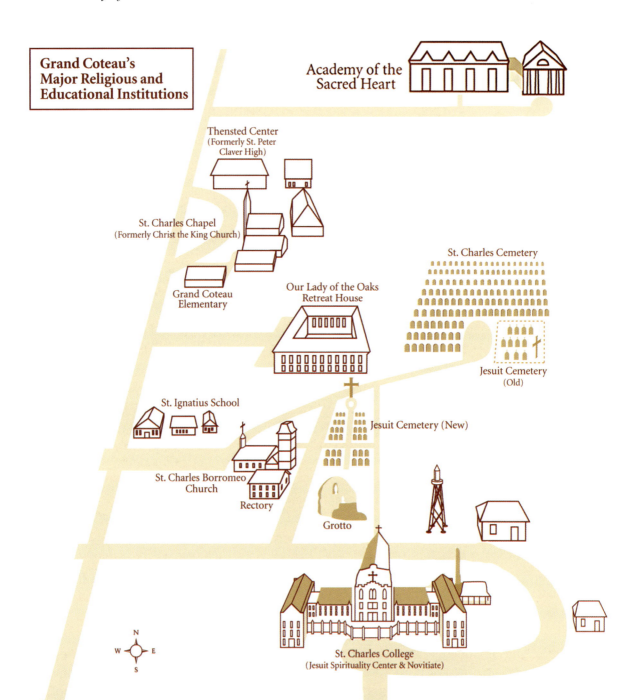

Missouri River valleys were severely affected by the Great Flood of 1927. While the Academy was not flooded by the raging waters, it was impacted, as the nuns welcomed evacuees from the flooded areas. Grand Coteau, which is French for "big ridge," or "big hill," fortunately is situated on high ground, at a much higher elevation than the land surrounding it. The Convent received and housed several families, while livestock, by the hundreds, grazed in the school's prairies and in those of nearby St. Charles College. The men and the vehicles of the College and the Convent were made available to the public charity. Fervent prayers increased each day after the Holy Mass and at the Blessing of the Holy Eucharist for the cessation of the terrible flooding.

It had been forecast that the floods would not stop until after mid-June. Concerned that they might not be able to reach the Academy, a number of parents took their daughters home in mid-May.

The father of one of the pupils had secured a rescue barge and used it to help a family taking refuge on the roof of their house in Prairie Lauren, about three miles away. The family would have perished without his help. Many acts of generosity and charity characterized the Academy and Grand Coteau communities during this time of natural catastrophe.

(A fuller account of the Great Flood of 1927, translated from the *House Journal 1926-1941* by Dr. Anna (Laurie) Servaes, can be found in the Appendix.)

Chapter 12

# Growth of 'The House of Grand Coteau'

The 20th century saw the construction of a number of new buildings on the campus of the Academy, as well as renovations and improvements of other structures. The growth of "The House of Grand Coteau," as it has been affectionately called by some, proved to be substantial, indeed.

As it approached its seventieth year, around 1905, the Bishop's Cottage was badly in need of repair. With the blessing of the Reverend Mother General, it was renovated with the express purpose of providing hospitality to the visiting bishop, Msgr. Rouxel, Auxiliary Bishop for Archbishop Chapelle. The nearby college of the Jesuits, having been in great part recently consumed by flames, could not, as in the past, offer hospitality to the bishop. Monseigneur felt quite at home in the cottage and seemed to enjoy the peaceful solitude. (Many years later, that same cottage would serve as a home for several of the Religious of the Sacred Heart, who later would move into a Community house in Grand Coteau.)

The chapel wing, which had been built in 1850, continued to undergo renovations over

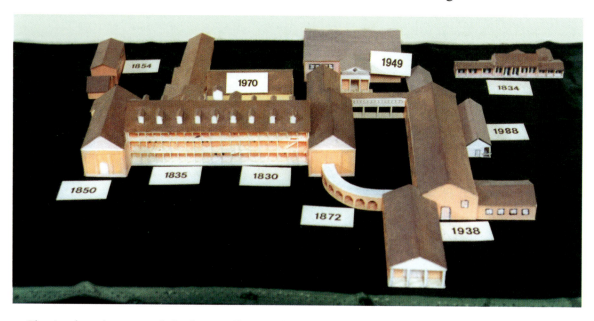

*The Academy has expanded substantially in its first two centuries, as shown in this model, which can be seen in the on-campus museum. The years showing refer to the dates in which the various buildings were constructed.*

the years, including the addition of the rooms to the right and left above the sanctuary. In the 1990s, Headmistress Carol Haggarty, RSCJ, oversaw the repainting of the interior and the addition of air-conditioning, to the great delight and comfort of students and faculty alike. The chapel remains in use by the school community and is often the site of alumnae weddings, as well as funerals.

In 1922, a new kitchen was built to replace the one recently destroyed by fire. This kitchen is in the same architectural style as the original one, which was built in 1834 by Samuel Young.

In 1938-39, Memorare Hall, done in the Greek Revival style, was designed and built by famed Louisiana architect A. Hays Town. The entryway is now graced by the handsome wrought iron and glass door, which came from the old Lapeyre home in New Orleans. The initial use of Memorare Hall was for the establishment of a college, which was in operation until 1956, when the thriving Academy took over all the available space. Academic classrooms and labs, the administration hall, and the auditorium are housed in Memorare Hall today. A curving staircase leads to the boarding area on the upper floor.

Originally, all Sacred Heart schools were boarding schools, but today the Academy in Grand Coteau is one of only two boarding schools in the Network of Sacred Heart Schools in

*Aerial view of the Academy of the Sacred Heart at Grand Coteau, taken sometime in the 1990s.*

the United States and Canada. It accepts girls from around the world or from just down the road.

The same year that Memorare Hall was completed, a brick arcade was added, connecting it to the library. The library, attached to the east end of the main building, bears features nearly identical to those of the chapel, on the west end, giving balance to the overall architectural design. There is some speculation that the library was built on part of the foundation of an earlier building because of differences in the bricks at the base of the building.

In 1949, the gymnasium was built. The bricks of the tornado-destroyed St. Michael's Convent of the Sacred Heart in Convent, Louisiana, were utilized in this construction. The gym is in use not only during the school day, but also for after-school basketball and volleyball games, as well as for sports clinics in the summer. The plaque on the gym reads:

*Much of the material used in this building was furnished from the Convent of St. Michael's, which was demolished in 1949. Thus is perpetuated the memory of the daughter convent by the mother that gave it birth.* (St. Michael's had been founded by the Academy's foundress, Mother Eugénie Audé, in 1825.)

In 1969-70, Latiolais Hall was built to house dining facilities. The dining hall gets lots of use and not only from students for lunch and the boarders for their daily meals. Many a faculty Christmas party has been enjoyed in this place, as well as faculty-parent potluck dinners. The III and IV Prep students have held yearly dances here and sometimes parents and teachers have met here for conferences. Latiolais Hall had been used as the site for Christmas at Coteau luncheons until the luncheons were relocated to a larger venue, and

*Rear view of the Academy shows the kitchen, the former first-floor dining hall with the museum on the floor above it, and the back side of the chapel and main building.*

*Growth of 'The House of Grand Coteau'* **65**

*The sanctuary in the chapel has undergone several changes in appearance over the decades.*

now vendors use the space to sell their wares during this holiday event. In times past, the building has hosted *congé* bingo games and Dad's Club dances, and it still hosts receptions for events such as Grandparents' Day, weddings, and funerals.

In 1985, a renovation of the beautiful gardens in front of the main building was conducted by the Academy Alumnae and Friends, and a wrought-iron fence was placed around them. Mrs. Karen McGlasson took charge of the project to restore the plants and shrubs damaged by a severe freeze in the early 1980s. *Lac Argile*, the original brick pit, was also restored in 1985.

For decades a statue of the Sacred Heart of Jesus has been a focal point of the garden. April of 2019 saw the installation of a new Carrara marble statue of the Sacred Heart, donated by Darrel J. Papillion, a parent, and his daughter to memorialize their recently deceased wife and mother, Shirley. His daughter Anna is a member of the bicentennial graduating class of 2021.

* * * * *

The Academy of the Sacred Heart, which was placed on the National Register of Historic Places in 1975, continues as an institution rich in history and tradition. The original 150 acres and wood-framed schoolhouse have developed into a thriving campus with numerous buildings and broad expanses of property, graced by the natural beauty of the countryside and the splendid avenues of oaks and pines.

Two centuries have passed, and still the verdant gardens, the iconic galleried building, the avenue of magnificent oaks, and the varied structures gracing the campus attract the attention of visitors, artists and historians, "*who find delight in the dignity, the originality of design, and the noble simplicity of the house of Grand Coteau.*" [1]

*The old barn, located behind the chapel, is a photogenic, rustic-looking structure that has served the Academy in one way or another since its construction in 1854. In 1914, it was badly damaged by fire and subsequently renovated.*

*Growth of 'The House of Grand Coteau'* **67**

Memorare Hall was built in 1938-39 to house the College of the Sacred Heart, which was in operation until 1956. The building now serves as the Academy's administrative headquarters, among other functions.

An elegant brick arcade, built in 1939, connects Memorare Hall with the library.

*This first-floor room in the main building served as a parlor for students and nuns alike before it was transformed into a classroom.*

*The layout of bookshelves and tables in this vintage photograph is quite different from the modern, computerized library of today.*

*Growth of 'The House of Grand Coteau'* **69**

*Latiolais Hall, built in 1969-70, functions primarily as a dining room but also as a multi-use place for events such as dances, receptions and Christmas at Coteau vending. Outside the hall is St. Francis patio (below), a gathering spot for students after lunch and during breaks between classes.*

*The layout of the formal gardens in the front yard of the main building has changed over the years, but the centerpiece has continued to be the statue of the Sacred Heart of Jesus.*

*Growth of 'The House of Grand Coteau'* **71**

*The formal gardens, renovated in 1985, retained their distinctive flower beds in the shapes of hearts, stars, circles and diamonds. The renovation was led by ASH alumna Mrs. Karen Veillon McGlasson.*

*Different versions of the Sacred Heart of Jesus statue have stood watch over the Academy almost since its inception.* **Left:** *Circa 1900, students gather at the base of the statue.* **Below:** *For decades this statue graced the formal gardens.* **Facing page:** *The new statue, made of Carrara marble and installed in 2019, was gifted to the Academy by a parent and his daughter, an ASH student.*

# Chapter 13

# Normal School and College of the Sacred Heart

In an effort to spread Madeleine Sophie's educational vision to post-secondary students, in 1914 the Academy established a State-accredited Normal School, which provided a two-year liberal arts education for women training to become teachers. Mother Mary Josephine Lynch, an able educator in Louisiana for nearly 20 years, was instrumental in founding the new school and provided a brief overview of its history:

*In 1914 the three schools in Louisiana – The Rosary, St. Michael's and Grand Coteau – formed one corporation empowered to give college credit for the first and second years; they quickly consolidated their programs as a Normal School at Grand Coteau. It gave invaluable service in preparing teachers for rural Louisiana. It was affiliated to the Catholic University of America as a four-year college in 1939, but could not gain standing with the Southern Association, the regional accrediting association. It closed in 1956 with an enrollment of forty students.* [1]

The distribution of the first diplomas given to graduates was in June of 1918, and by then the Normal School was experiencing growth and success. In March of 1925, the chairman of the Board of Examiners required of the Normal School full information about its Course of Studies, the qualifications of the professors, and details about the practice-teaching. In May, the administration received the revised Course of Study for the State teacher-training colleges, a revision that did not call for any radical changes in their academic courses. The Course of Studies, a liberal arts course – including religion, philosophy, English, history, Latin, modern languages, and mathematics – easily met with the approval of the State Board of Education.

The Normal School had strict rules governing the behavior of its students, as explained in its Recommendations:

*1. A quiet, refined manner and voice are urged at all times, especially during Academy classes and on Academy premises.*

*2. It is unbecoming to sit on window sills, desks, tables, etc.*

*3. One should not undress without drawing window curtains.*

*4. Lounging on beds is altogether out of place at any time. When several gather in a room, bring chairs. It is undignified to sprawl about on the lawns and benches.* [2]

Accompanying those Recommendations were Disciplinary Regulations:

*1. Silence is required a) In the library b) In chapel c) At the times indicated elsewhere.*

*2. Candy may be kept in rooms and desk, provided it is enclosed in tin boxes.*

*3. All furniture must not be marred; no room injuries; nor walls or door marked; no library books defaced or used uncovered.* [3]

Students interested in the performing arts had ample opportunity to become involved in theatrical productions. The plays presented – "Two Naughty Old Ladies," "Her Son's Sweetheart," and "Fabiola," for example – as well as Christmas plays and French and English comedies earned enough money to help furnish various classrooms and to give annual gifts to the school. [4]

* * * * *

Change was in the air in the early months of 1939, not only for the Normal School, but for a world on the brink of war.

On April 23, 1939, an elaborate celebration heralded the coming of the new College of the Sacred Heart with the blessing and dedication of Memorare Hall. Twenty-three guests from the Academy's sister-school in New Orleans began arriving around 10:30 in the morning. Others in attendance included 35 priests, three Roman prelates, a number of religious from different orders, friends, family, and students. At 3 p.m. Bishop Jeanmard began in the Chapel, followed by a procession of approximately 1,500 people through Pine Alley and into the garden. The Bishop led the crowd in prayer by the front door, then blessed the Crucifix near the main corridor. Many in the crowd gathered in Memorare Hall, and guest speakers were introduced.

The first speaker, District Attorney Austin Fontenot, praised the institution that had produced excellent results for education and morality for more than 115 uninterrupted years, despite the Civil War, epidemics, and the Depression.

When the Bishop took the podium, he announced that the Normal School had now become a State-accredited four-year college. The College would be able to award diplomas in Baccalaureate of Sciences, of Arts, and of Commerce. [5]

On September 12, 1939, the College opened with 57 students. World War II, which had begun on September 1, when Nazi Germany invaded Poland, would impact the lives of the students and faculty; however, classes would continue both in the College and in the Academy.

On November 24, 1940, nearly 7,000 people participated in a procession to Grand Coteau on the Feast of Christ the King to pray for peace in the world, as had been ordered for Catholics worldwide by Pope Pius XII.

Students at the College had many opportunities to participate in various clubs and activities. The honor society, the Accolades, would choose a topic, such as Louisiana, for further study and discussion. The Coteau Choristers performed at various area schools and clubs, and the Footlighters entertained audiences with rollicking comedies and dramatic plays. The Press Club took responsibility for both *Coteau Columns* newspaper and the *Memorare* yearbook. Students were able to join the International Relations Club, the Students' Welfare Association, the French Club, the Coteau Athletic Association, and Sigma Delta Pi, which was the Hispanic Honor Society.

Organizations to enhance one's spiritual life included the Children of Mary, described as "*...the Society in the world, sharers in the work of spreading the love of Christ.*" [6] Other groups were the Promoters, who worked to spread devotion to the Sacred Heart

*The College of the Sacred Heart as it appeared in an early brochure designed to recruit new students, circa 1940... It shows Memorare Hall and the dormitory, with "Mirror Lake" in the foreground.*

of Jesus, and the National Federation of Catholic College Students. Recognizing that a sound mind often accompanies a sound body, the College provided various athletic opportunities, including equestrian arts, tennis, and volleyball.

Many older residents of Acadiana were taught by an alumna of the Normal School or College of the Sacred Heart, as many women attended the school for its excellence in teacher training and in spirituality during its 42 years of existence. As its reputation grew, the college was affiliated to the Catholic University of America in 1939. On September 7, 1953, the College admitted two Black students, marking the beginning of desegregation in the Society's Southern schools.

Despite the enthusiasm, hard work, and good spirit, the College had only a few years of existence remaining. With deep sorrow and regret, on January 25, 1956, it was announced that the College was closing at the end of the current school year. Reasons given included a shortage of students committed to Catholic higher education, inconvenient distance from any city, and the need for more space for a growing Academy. The final commencement exercises were held on May 31, 1956, with Bishop Jules Jeanmard presiding over the ceremony and Fr. Auguste Coyle, SJ, chaplain at the school, giving the final commencement address.

\* \* \* \* \*

A former student at the College shared her memories, saying she was happy to tell a little of the wonderful four years she spent in the College. Mary Pat Rives, RSCJ, started attending classes in 1942 and graduated with a BA in 1946.

*I was at the Rosary (New Orleans) in 1941..., and as I thought of college I chose Coteau as it was closer to San Antonio, Texas, where I lived. The college had been a normal school and moved into a four year college with a very good reputation. The*

*Society sent a number of very good and qualified Religious to be on the faculty.*

*My major was English and Education. The student body lived on campus, with some going home on weekends, and so classes were held during the week days.*

*My favorite memory: dear friends from Louisiana, other states and Mexico in addition to a strong curriculum.*

*The war years took a toll on the college student body but in time with the close of the college it gave room for the Academy to grow and prosper.* [7]

Theresa Moser, RSCJ, did not graduate from College of the Sacred Heart since it closed the third year she was there. Instead, she finished at Maryville College in St. Louis, Missouri, after she entered the Society of the Sacred Heart in the autumn of 1956. After teaching in Ohio and California, she served in the academic administration at the University of San Francisco and pastoral administration at St. Ignatius Parish and as a member of the Provincial Team. She submitted the following description of her years at the College:

*I was at CSH (College of the Sacred Heart) Grand Coteau from Fall 1953 to Spring 1956. The oldest of nine children – with eight other siblings to go to college at my parents' expense – I accepted the scholarship [to attend CSH].*

*I took the usual courses, with a degree in English in mind and some education courses for a possible teaching career. I especially remember a class in the history of drama taught by Marjory Erskine, RSCJ.*

*A favorite memory involves four students from St. Louis (Maryville) who came for one year ... in my sophomore year. They were the Trout twins, Lily and Ginny, Jane Bourke, and Colette Pezolt (I think that was her name). They spent all breaks between classes playing bridge in the small college smoking lounge. My roommate was Carmen Diaz, who knew not to speak to me before I had had my morning coffee. I am still friends with Jane and Carmen. The college was small, about 50 students, so we knew everyone. There was not much to do off campus except go to Sunset for coffee or Lafayette for occasional distraction. The closest other institution was the Jesuit retreat house in Grand Coteau.*

*In my third year it was announced that the college was to be closed at the end of the year. Some students organized to try to save it, but I didn't think that was likely. So, I had to think of my future. Finish somewhere else, like Manhattanville or Maryville? I decided instead to enter the Society of the Sacred Heart.* [8]

Another graduate of the College is Gladys Richard Wheat Chachere, who was born September 14, 1915, in the country area of south Louisiana known as Buzzard's Roost. The great-great-great niece of Charles Smith, whose gift of property allowed for the foundation of the Academy, Gladys seemed destined to attend the school. The generosity and hospitality of her Uncle John and Aunt Blanche Smith enabled her to live near enough to the Academy to walk to school, just a mile from where she lived. She remembered the nuns and boarders at the College, but not much more, perhaps due to her being 104 when she was interviewed about her experiences at Sacred Heart. At the time, she was still reading the paper daily and attending Mass weekly.

# Chapter 14

# The World War II Years

In September of 1939 the new and returning students to the schools operated by the Religious of the Sacred Heart in Grand Coteau numbered 120 in the Parish School, 186 at the Colored School, 56 in the College, 49 boarders in the Academy, and 3 who were not boarders. They might have had some knowledge that their *rentrée* coincided with the Nazi invasion of Poland on September 1, but it is unlikely that many would have predicted that World War II would last six long years.

While the war would not have an immediate, devastating effect on the day-to-day operations of the schools, it would impact their prayer life and their resolve to participate in war efforts and simply to endure. By October, prayers would be increased: *"We double up our Aves in this month to obtain the Peace for the world plunged in the distress by the European war."* [1]

*Holocaust hero Fr. Ernest Joseph Burrus, S.J., gave a riveting anti-Nazi talk to the faculty and students at the Academy in 1940. The previous year, he had been labeled* persona non grata *and expelled from Austria by the Gestapo for helping Jews escape the country. He was also known for having smuggled Pope Pius XI's encyclical "With Burning Concern" from Italy into Switzerland for publication. A renowned scholar and prolific author, he had entered the Jesuit Novitiate in Grand Coteau in 1925 and was teaching at the Novitiate when he gave the talk at the Academy.*

During the month of February of 1940, the Committee of Education sent subsidies to provide hot meals for the children of needy families, and a kitchen was organized at the Colored School, where more than 150 children were fed daily meals. The Parish School enjoyed the same benefit.

On March 19, 1940, Fr. Joseph Burrus, SJ, a teacher at St. Charles College, gave a lecture on the horrors of the Nazi regime, something he had already witnessed firsthand. Fr. Burrus had been expelled from Austria by the National Socialists in 1939 after he helped Austrian Jews escape. Despite Nazi efforts to silence him, he also helped preserve the Word of God by smuggling Pope Pius XI's encyclical *With Burning Concern* from Italy into Switzerland for publication. Considered a Holocaust hero, he was unafraid to speak truth to power and to share what he had witnessed with interested audiences, which included both faculty and students at the Academy and College.

At the May 13, 1940, celebration of the beatification

of Mother Rose Philippine Duchesne, the homilist, Fr. David Durham, SJ, expounded on three traits of Blessed Philippine that were characteristic of her life: an ideal student, a sustained generosity, and a heroic courage. He noted that she had showed these virtues in all phases of her life, and that the youth of today could aspire to these traits, particularly *"courageous generosity in the middle of the perils and dangers of the present hour."* [2] A year later, a three-day celebration of her beatification, involving many of the local clergy and religious, was highlighted by veneration of the relic of the Blessed Philippine.

The first American Legion Award was presented at the Prizes event in June of 1940 in recognition of the caliber of education received by our students – *"education that forms the character and prepares them to 'service' of the nation."* [3] October 10 saw the blessing of the new statue of *Mater Admirabilis*, a happy day.

\* \* \* \* \*

Like Americans everywhere, the ASH community was shocked to hear the announcement that Japan had attacked Pearl Harbor on December 7, 1941, causing 2,403 fatalities and the destruction of many American ships and planes. That attack propelled America into war against Japan. Then, on December 11, Congress declared war against Germany, just hours after Germany declared war on the U.S. The country was now at war on two fronts. The Coteau Community responded by imploring Mary, the Immaculate Mother, whose feast of the Immaculate Conception had just been observed on December 8, to *"protect the nation that is devoted to her."* [4]

With the United States now involved in the war, 1942 saw a decline in numbers at the Sacred Heart-Grand Coteau schools and retreats due to women enlisting in various branches of the Armed Services and attendant difficulties in transportation. The transportation challenges were due in part to the rationing of supplies and goods necessitated by the ongoing war effort.

In February, Reverend Mother Mary Fitzwilliam asked the community to choose a day of this month in which each would make a Holy Hour and undertake *"some penitent practices in union with the flow of prayers in the entire world in order to obtain the end of the current conflicts."* [5]

February 8 saw the inauguration of a new regulation: year-round Daylight Savings Time. This was signed into law by President Franklin Roosevelt for the remainder of the war as a national defense measure to conserve energy.

By the end of March, Mr. Ashton LeCompte gave a demonstration of the procedures to follow in case of aerial bombardments. He emphasized that the main thing was to remain calm, to follow the given recommendations, and to respond to the different signals given as warnings. He explained what these signals meant and also instructed how to remedy injuries from different types of gas, which could be more or less dangerous.

The on-going war caused hardship for the small community of Grand Coteau, including the members of the Academy. The early days of May of 1942 saw residents of the town and the convent school registering for sugar rations.

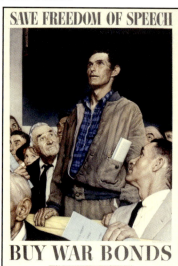

*With the U.S. at war in Europe and in the Pacific Theatre, an* esprit de corps *prevailed throughout the country as people banded together to support the war effort. Posters backing U.S. troops and promoting the purchase of War Bonds were plastered everywhere: in public buildings, bus stations, private businesses, even in some educational institutions.*

By September 23, 1942, the Academy had enrolled 66 boarding school pupils, while the College had 72 students and one part-time boarder. By 1943, the Academy community was supplying food for the Colored School because the government no longer could. February of 1944 saw patriotic celebrations for the sale of War Bonds held in the area, and a banquet offered to the mothers of soldiers as well as to former students of the Colored School.

A terse entry for June 6, 1944 – D-Day – called for a *"day of intense prayers for the success of the European invasion by the Allies."* [6]

By September 28, 1944, there were 72 students in the College and 86 at the Academy. The Lord granted the Community's many prayers by filling the schools, so much so that the administration had to refuse several children due to lack of space. The tide of the war was turning as the Allies occupied more territories and countries once under the rule and domination of the Nazis in the European Theatre and the Japanese in the Pacific Theatre.

With the end of the war in sight, the world learned of the death of President Franklin Delano Roosevelt on April 12, 1945. *"Let us pray for his soul and for the country,"* an entry in the *House Journal* stated. [7]

Finally, on VE Day (Victory in Europe) – May 8, 1945 – the end of the war in Europe was proclaimed by President Harry Truman. To celebrate, the Sacred Heart schools held a *congé*. A few months later, on August 19, on the order of the Bishop and President Truman, the schools celebrated a day of thanksgiving to commemorate the end of the war with Japan. Adoration of the Very Blessed Sacrament (*Très Saint Sacrement*) was observed and a communal rosary was prayed. And as another reminder that the war was truly over, *"on September 30, the nation's clocks were set back an hour to take back the natural course of the day."* [8]

A good number of worshipers ended the year and began this one (1946) at the feet of Jesus at the Tabernacle in a feeling of thanksgiving for the end of this terrible world war, and in intense prayers to obtain a lasting and cordial peace between the nations.

*Mother Henriette Delille, once described as "the humble servant of slaves," was renowned for her profound acts of mercy toward formerly enslaved people who were penniless, homeless and dying on the streets of antebellum New Orleans. In 1842, she founded the Sisters of the Holy Family, who took over the teaching duties at St. Peter Claver School in Grand Coteau from the Sacred Heart nuns in 1947. In the 1940s and '50s, dozens of women of African descent from the Grand Coteau-Opelousas-Lafayette area joined the Sisters of the Holy Family. Mother Delille was named "Servant of God" by the Church in 1989 and was being seriously considered for canonization before the dawn of the 21st century.*

---

*The last months were marked and blessed by a great outpouring of charity among all our houses, and our students competed generously to send abundant provisions of supplies and useful objects not only to our religious families, but also to the families of the religious. May the Lord bless and reward his family of Coteau for its charity toward the victims [in] Europe!* [9]

\* \* \* \* \*

The years following the end of World War II and before the Second Vatican Council were reflective of a return to "normalcy" for the Sacred Heart-Grand Coteau communities. These years of growth and re-adjustment were marked by many changes, including new construction and the acquisition of various needed items. Excerpts illustrating some of those changes are taken from the *House Journal 1941-1953*, as follows:

**September, 1945:** *That September there were 92 in the College; 85 in the Academy.*

**September 15, 1946:** *We considerably enlarged the Cottage to house the eight secular school teachers. We also extended the annex of the Refectory where the electric washer is located. We arranged the armoires coming from St. Michael's there. His Excellency Mgsr. Jeanmard makes a gift of the great / big statue of the Sacred Heart, which will be at the back of the chapel. The new Stations of the Way of the Cross were also offered by generous friends.*

**March 14, 1947:** *The Stations and the big Crucifix were installed in the Chapel.* [10]

**May 1, 1947:** *Day of prayer for the conversion of Russia. Processions in the parishes. Here, we have a formal and patriotic Holy Hour, begun by the national hymn, preached by the Reverend Father Coyle. Rosary, songs, address (short speeches), ended by the song "Holy God."* [11]

**May 30, 1947:** *From now on, the Colored School that our Mothers directed for more than 80 years, is ceded, by decision of our First Mothers, to the Parish of Christ the King, and will be administered by the Sisters of the Holy Family of New Orleans, into which about 30 of our former students have entered.* [12]

Chapter 15

# The Impact of Vatican II

The second half of the 20$^{th}$ century was a time of post-war prosperity and growth as higher education became more accessible due in part to the G.I. Bill, allowing returning servicemen and women to pursue college educations. The decades following the end of World War II were also a time of social and sexual revolution, student protests against the Vietnam War, widespread drug use, men on the moon, political assassinations, the Watergate scandal, and – especially significant to Roman Catholics – the Second Vatican Council.

Catholics worldwide were greatly influenced and changed by the convocation of the world's bishops and theologians called by Pope John XXIII on January 25, 1959, and convened on October 11, 1962, and ended on December 8, 1965. The convocation, commonly referred to as Vatican II, sought to make the Catholic Church more relevant to the lives of Catholics in every nation in an irreversibly industrialized world.

Its impact certainly was felt by the Religious of the Sacred Heart and transformed the lives of both the nuns and students of the Academy in Grand Coteau. The RSCJs were among the religious communities that changed their habits to a modified, simpler habit, then gradually adopted modern, contemporary dress.

A major change occurred when the RSCJs removed the rule of cloister in 1964, allowing the members more access to the everyday world and further outreach to the marginalized citizens of the Grand Coteau area and beyond. Students became more involved in social outreach, especially at the Thensted Center, where they tutored, organized various holiday parties, and sponsored Saturday Play Days. But perhaps the biggest impact of Vatican II on

*A common sight on the grounds of the Academy for decades, this traditional floor-length habit became a thing of the past for many nuns after Vatican II. Some opted to continue wearing the habit or a modified version of it.*

*The Thensted Outreach Center in Grand Coteau was founded in 1982 by Sr. Margaret "Mike" Hoffman, RSCJ, after her community's rule of cloister was lifted in the wake of Vatican II. Religious sisters and students alike followed in her footsteps, becoming involved in social outreach activities that were, and still are, coordinated through this Center. (The building previously housed St. Peter Claver High School for Black children.)*

every Catholic was that Mass would no longer be said in Latin. Now the priest would pray the Mass in the vernacular – English, in the U.S. – and he would be facing the congregation!

As these changes were gradually absorbed into the everyday life of Catholics, the various North American schools founded by the Society became the Network of Sacred Heart Schools, which number 25 schools in the U.S and Canada. In the 1980s, Sr. Susan Maxwell, RSCJ, the Director of the Network, while attending a national meeting of educators in Washington, D.C., was singled out by a Department of Education official, who confided in her that she oversaw *the finest chain of schools in the nation*. One of the reasons for that accolade must have been the Goals and Criteria, the guiding principles and standards for every Network school.

\* \* \* \* \*

Among the main changes at the Academy in the latter part of the 20$^{th}$ century was an explosion of technology. While the founding mothers would not recognize the computers and robots now in the school were they to visit today, they would surely see the same industry, creativity, and commitment to quality education that have always been hallmarks of the Academy.

That commitment led the Board of Trustees and the Administration to extend the school into the lower grades in 1987. The Primary School occupies most of the first floor of the iconic main building and has added a new liveliness and energy to the campus.

84 *Academy of the Sacred Heart at Grand Coteau*

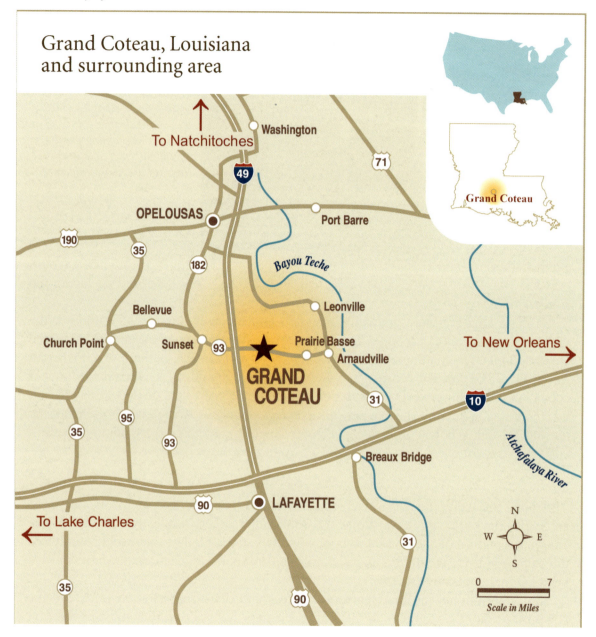

Map shows Grand Coteau area in the latter part of the 20th century, including the nearby Interstate highway, I-49. The system of roads serving the region has come a long way since Mother Audé and Sister Layton rode into town on horseback on a dirt road in the summer of 1821.

# Part III

# Onward to the 21st Century

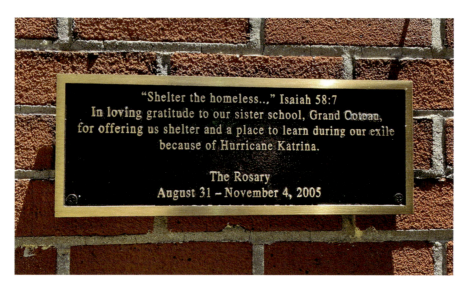

*To show their gratitude for providing "a home away from home" in the wake of Hurricane Katrina, "The Rosary" family gifted their Coteau sister-school with a plaque quoting Isaiah 58:7.*

# Chapter 16

# Sacred Heart GOALS and CRITERIA

One outcome of Vatican II that significantly impacted the Society of the Sacred Heart was the call to decide whether the Society was to be contemplative (monastic) or apostolic, while also becoming more de-centralized.

By giving up some of the characteristics of monastic life, such as the rule of cloister and the recitation of the Office, the Society was able to be both contemplative and apostolic and achieved de-centralization by engaging more lay teachers and providing more outreach services in their communities. However, this de-centralization also raised the concern of the Schools of the Sacred Heart losing the very essence of a Sacred Heart education. Therefore, the U.S. Provincial established a task force of both Religious and lay faculty to capture and preserve that essence.

The work of the task force resulted in the first edition of the Goals and Criteria, in 1975, and in the establishment of the Network Commission on Goals (NCOG). The commission was put in charge of designing and implementing a system of individual schools' accountability for living the Society's mission of education.

This process was re-visioned in 1990 and again in 2005. The re-named Commission became the Sacred Heart Commission on Goals, and it remains the avenue for reflection on how each school lives out the Goals and Criteria. The Schools of the Sacred Heart, the RSCJ Community, and the Commission on Goals began a revision of the Goals and Criteria in 2019. This final draft was submitted to the Provincial Team of the United States-Canada Province and was approved December 22, 2020. While the Goals remained the same, the Criteria were updated. They are included below as the 2020 version following the 2005 version that is familiar to long-time Academy members.

The Goals and Criteria provide the foundation that leads a Network school community to "*a hope that believes in the goodness of each individual, a hope that believes in the goodness of humanity, a hope that believes in and trusts the love of the Heart of God.*" [1]

## Foundational Principles

1. In the Goals and Criteria, the Society of the Sacred Heart defines the mission of the school as part of the Society's educational mission in the Catholic Church.

2. Each school is accountable to the Society of the Sacred Heart Commission on Goals for adherence to the Goals and Criteria.

3. Each school's Board of Trustees and Administration establish and uphold policies that are consistent with the Goals and Criteria.

4. The school allocates its resources to support each Goal and its Criteria.

5. The school is in compliance with professional standards as stated by accrediting agencies.

# Goal I

## Schools of the Sacred Heart commit themselves to educate to a personal and active faith in God.

- Rooted in the love of Jesus Christ, the school promotes a personal relationship with God and fosters the spiritual lives of its members.
- The school seeks to form its students in the attitudes of the heart of Jesus, expressed in respect, compassion, forgiveness and generosity.
- The entire school program explores one's relationship to God, to self, to others, and to all creation.
- Opening themselves to the transforming power of the Spirit of God, members of the school community engage in personal and communal prayer, reflection and action.
- The entire school program affirms that there is meaning and value in life and fosters a sense of hope in the individual and in the school community.
- The school fosters inter-religious acceptance and dialogue by educating to an understanding of and deep respect for the religions of the world.
- The school presents itself to the wider community as a Christ-centered institution and as an expression of the mission of the Society of the Sacred Heart.

## 2020 Criteria for Goal I

- The school identifies itself to the wider community as a Catholic-independent Sacred Heart School and embodies the mission of the Society of the Sacred Heart.
- The school forms its student and adult members in attitudes of the heart of Jesus, such as gratitude, generosity, compassion and forgiveness.
- The school community reflects an ethos of joy, hope and celebration, and its programs assert that there is meaning and value in life.
- The school community welcomes and respects persons of all faiths and educates to an understanding of the religious and spiritual traditions of the world.
- School leadership prioritizes space and time for silence and contemplation for its members to deepen their interior life.
- Members of the school community, open to the transforming power of the Spirit of God, engage in personal and communal prayer, discernment and reflection which inform their actions.
- The school community, rooted in the love of Jesus Christ, nurtures the spiritual lives of its members through the exploration of one's relationship to God, to self, to others and to creation.

## Goal II

**Schools of the Sacred Heart commit themselves
to educate to a deep respect for intellectual values.**

• The school develops and implements a curriculum based on the Goals and Criteria, educational research and ongoing evaluation.

• The school provides a rigorous education that incorporates all forms of critical thinking and inspires a life-long love of learning.

• The school program develops aesthetic values and the creative use of the imagination.

• The faculty utilizes a variety of teaching and learning strategies that recognizes the individual needs of the students.

• The school provides ongoing professional development for faculty and staff.

• Members of the school community model and teach ethical and respectful use of technology.

### 2020 Criteria for Goal II

• Sacred Heart educators and students engage in challenging experiences that inspire intellectual curiosity, a global mindset and a life-long love of learning.

• Sacred Heart educators develop and implement a dynamic curriculum, effective instructional methodology, current educational research, and ongoing evaluation.

• Sacred Heart educators and students utilize a variety of teaching and learning strategies to support their growth and development.

• The school curricular and co-curricular programs integrate innovation and collaboration, critical thinking and problem-solving, the exploration of emerging technologies and critical evaluation of information.

• The school utilizes space and the physical environment in alignment with best pedagogical practices.

• The school cultivates aesthetic values and the creative use of the imagination.

• Sacred Heart educators assume responsibility for their professional growth, supported by resources and a culture that promotes life-long learning.

## Goal III

**Schools of the Sacred Heart commit themselves
to educate to a social awareness which impels to action.**

• The school educates to a critical consciousness that leads its total community to analyze and reflect on the values of society and to act for justice.

• The school offers all its members opportunities for direct service and advocacy and instills a life-long commitment to service.

• The school is linked in a reciprocal manner with ministries among people who are poor, marginalized and suffering from injustice.

• In our multicultural world, the school prepares and inspires students to be active, informed, and responsible citizens locally, nationally, and globally.

• The school teaches respect for creation and prepares students to be stewards of the earth's resources.

### 2020 Criteria for Goal III

• Sacred Heart educators prepare students to serve the common good in an interdependent world.

• Sacred Heart educators immerse students in diverse global perspectives, developing competencies such as critical consciousness, language facility and cultural literacy.

• The school, drawing from Catholic Social Teaching, educates students to analyze and work to eradicate social structures, practices, systems, and values that perpetuate racism and other injustices.

• All members of the school community accept accountability for the care of God's creation, practice effective stewardship of the earth's resources, and work to alleviate the climate crisis.

• School programs promote informed active citizenship and civic responsibility on the local, national and global level.

• The school community engages in direct service, advocacy, outreach and partnership to work for justice, peace and the integrity of creation.

• Sacred Heart educators work to develop in the students a life-long commitment to service.

## Goal IV

### Schools of the Sacred Heart commit themselves
### to educate to the building of community as a Christian value.

• The school implements an ongoing plan for educating both adults and students in the heritage and mission of Sacred Heart education.

• The school promotes a safe and welcoming environment in which each person is valued, cared for and respected.

• Adult members of the school model and teach skills needed to build community and practice clear, direct and open communication.

• The school has programs that teach the principles of nonviolence, conflict resolution and peacemaking.

• The school makes a deliberate effort to recruit students and employ faculty and staff of diverse races, ethnicities and backgrounds.

• The financial aid program effectively supports socioeconomic diversity.

• The school participates actively in the national and international Networks of Sacred Heart schools.

## 2020 Criteria for Goal IV

• The school, affirming that all are created in the image and likeness of God, promotes the inherent dignity of the human person and strives for relationships characterized by inclusion and mutual respect.

• The school implements an ongoing plan for educating all members of the community to the charism, mission and heritage of the Society of the Sacred Heart.

• The school engages with the Network of Sacred Heart Schools in the United States and Canada and Sacred Heart schools around the world.

• All members of the school community support a clean, healthy and safe environment.

• Members of the school community practice and teach with a spirit of peace and reconciliation the principles of non-violence and conflict management.

• School leadership demonstrates a conscious effort to recruit students and employ faculty and staff of diverse races, ethnicities and backgrounds.

• School leadership allocates financial resources to support socio-economic diversity both in the admission process and in the daily lives of students.

# Goal V

**Schools of the Sacred Heart commit themselves
to educate to personal growth in an atmosphere of wise freedom.**

• All members of the school community show respect, acceptance and concern for themselves and for others.

• School policies and practices promote self-discipline, responsible decision-making, and accountability.

• Students grow in self-knowledge and develop self-confidence as they learn to deal realistically with their gifts and limitations.

• School programs provide for recognizing, nurturing and exercising leadership in its many forms.

• The school provides opportunities for all members of the community to share their knowledge and gifts with others.

• All members of the school community take personal responsibility for balance in their lives and for their health and well-being.[2]

## 2020 Criteria for Goal V

• Student and adult members of the school community grow in courage and confidence as they discover new abilities, cultivate strengths, learn from mistakes, develop empathy, and exercise resilience in meeting challenges.

• All members of the school community take personal responsibility for health and balance in their lives, supported by a school culture that promotes spiritual, intellectual, physical and social-emotional well-being.

- Members of the school community model and teach respectful dialogue in support of clear, direct, open communication.
- All members of the school community endeavor to practice informed ethical decision-making and accountability.
- Student and adult members of the school community model, practice, and teach safe, ethical and responsible use of technology.
- Sacred Heart educators cultivate in the students life skills, such as initiative, creativity and agility.
- Sacred Heart schools recognize and educate to motivational, inspirational, and transformational leadership.

# Chapter 17

# Toward a Noble Future

Hurricane Katrina brought a new set of challenges for the Academy in September of 2005, when New Orleans evacuees sought admission to the school. Nearly 350 girls from various schools in the stricken area, including "The Rosary," a Network of Sacred Heart Schools sister-school, were absorbed into Coteau's student population, nearly doubling the enrollment. Temporary school buildings were found nearby and many Academy families provided housing for students, teachers, and staff from New Orleans. For more than two months, the Rosary evacuees found a safe haven in Grand Coteau, and the Academy community had a real-life opportunity to live the values expressed in the Goals and Criteria.

The autumn of 2008 saw the school on the receiving end when Hurricane Gustav hit the area and severely damaged the campus. Nearly every building was damaged and the electricity was out for a week. The loss of the historic cistern that had graced the back entrance to the main building was felt deeply by the community. Students, parents, faculty, staff, and alumnae came to help restore the campus to its natural beauty, again realizing a first-hand opportunity to live the Goals and Criteria, especially Goals III and IV: service and the building of community.

A long-contemplated and historic change occurred on the campus of the Academy of the Sacred Heart in 2006: the opening of St. John Berchmans school for boys. The establishment of this new school marked the fulfillment of Charles and Mary Smith's original idea of providing single-gender education for both boys and girls.

After a name change in 2011 to Berchmans Academy, an upper-level division was added by opening a ninth grade,

*Berchmans Academy opened on the Grand Coteau campus in 2006, offering single-gender education to boys and young men.*

*The monster storm named Hurricane Katrina hit land on the Louisiana-Mississippi coast on August 29, 2005, causing the flooding of 75 to 80% of New Orleans. As a result, students and teachers from "The Rosary" sought safe haven at ASH-Coteau and remained here for more than two months before returning to the Crescent City.*

with a next-level class added each year through grade 12. Since 2006, the Academy and Berchmans have operated as Schools of the Sacred Heart.

Berchmans Academy was established as a result of the gift of portable buildings to house the classrooms and administrative offices, a gift that was made possible in the wake of Hurricane Katrina. An ASH-Coteau alumna on the board of a Philadelphia private school had heard about the generosity of the Academy to the many young women displaced by the hurricane. With open arms, ASH had welcomed girls not only from "the Rosary," a sister school in New Orleans, but also schoolgirls from other hard-hit, flooded areas of the Gulf Coast.

This act inspired the alumna to petition her board to donate the portable buildings that had been used on their Pennsylvania campus during the construction of new buildings. Seeing no further need for these portable buildings and recognizing that ASH-Coteau had a need for more classroom space, the board donated the buildings. These became the foundation of Berchmans Academy and allowed for the new school to become a reality, no more just a long-held dream – often requested as early as September of 1830 – for many parents desirous of the same stellar education for their sons as their daughters enjoyed.

Advances in technology prompted the Academy to implement a Tablet PC program in 2007, in part as an outcome of the extended power outage that resulted from Hurricane Gustav. With such a program, the faculty and students can continue their education with instruction during extended closings, as was the case during the Covid-19 quarantine that began in March of 2020.

Most classrooms have Smart Board technology, and all students have access to desktop computers, laptops, or tablets. Their use is embedded in the curriculum with an emphasis on creation and engineering as well as word processing and slideshows. A robotics program and a 3-D printer have excited the imagination of many a student and allowed for opportunities to tinker, imagine, and create. The school continues to be committed to ongoing professional development for faculty in the integration of the technology for the 21$^{st}$ century at all grade levels.

One much-appreciated improvement in the early 21$^{st}$ century was the installation of updated air-conditioning and heating, not only in the main buildings, but also in the chapel. This was accomplished in 2008 as the boiler system and the window AC units in the main building were replaced.

\* \* \* \* \*

After two centuries of educating young women, the Academy of the Sacred Heart welcomes the challenges of a third century, replete with ever-evolving technology and educational practices. One such challenge occurred during the Covid-19 pandemic that began in 2020. During the opening days of the 2020-21 academic year, students had a blend of in-class instruction and distance learning. By mid-September the school was able to accommodate all students with daily in-class instruction, while following the State's mandated guidelines

*The iconic cistern, which stood near the back entrance to the main building for many decades, was destroyed in 2008 by the merciless winds of Hurricane Gustav.*

*Students were not allowed to attend school in person for several months during the height of the Covid-19 pandemic of 2020, by order of the State of Louisiana. But the SSH students were there in spirit, as these photos in the Chapel of St. John Berchmans will attest.*

as well as the high standards of a Network School of the Sacred Heart.[1]

On August 26, 2020, Hurricane Laura, with 150-miles-per-hour winds, inflicted catastrophic damage on southwestern Louisiana. As the Academy did after Hurricane Katrina in 2005, the Schools of the Sacred Heart welcomed students from the hurricane-ravaged western parishes. Six girls and seven boys joined the Upper Schools and Lower Schools by September 1. Residing with local families and friends or staying in rentals, some students were able to return home by the end of September while others stayed for a longer period.

What remains constant and unchanging at the Academy of the Sacred Heart in Grand Coteau is the commitment to the Goals and Criteria and the mission of revealing God's love. As Sr. Tippy Guillory, RSCJ, once said:

"We can't fail; we are doing God's work!"

\* \* \* \* \*

For two centuries God has held the Academy of the Sacred Heart in the palm of His hand, seeing it through fires, fevers, floods, hurricanes, wars, and pandemics. A Louisiana treasure, the now-named Schools of the Sacred Heart look forward to the future. Drawing upon a rich history, SSH embraces the challenge and privilege of preparing students who will make contributions to a better world, who with aims and ideals will make the future noble.

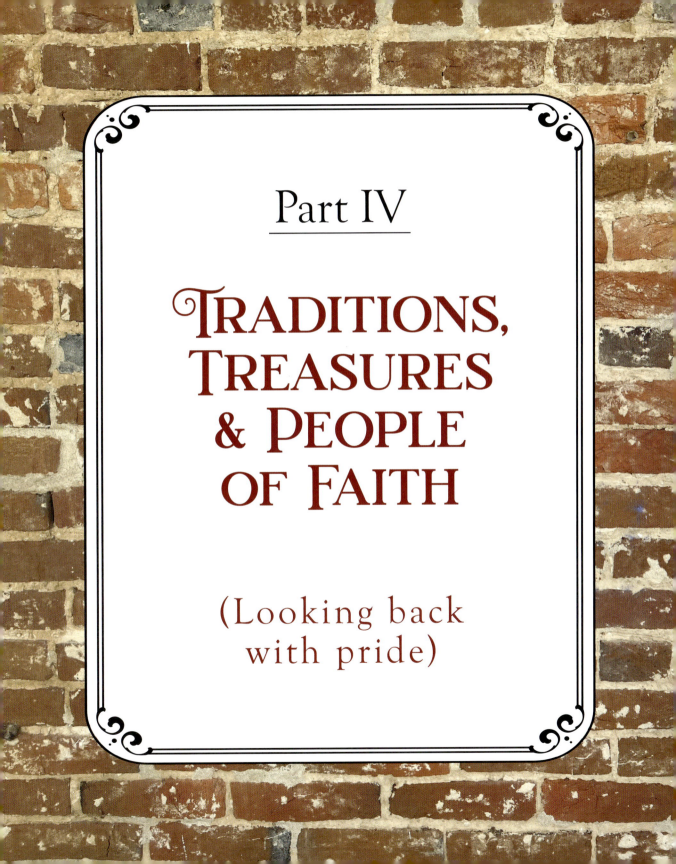

*Prayer in the chapel is among the more solemn and memorable traditions of the Academy. Praying before Mass in the late 1950s are Mary Burns (left) and Peggy Guidry, both in the Class of 1959. Ms. Burns would later serve as Headmistress of the school, from 2002 to 2007.*

# Chapter 18

# Traditions, Customs & Activities

The early years of the Academy saw the establishment of many customs and traditions, some of which no longer occur, but many that are still much-treasured by alumnae, students, parents, faculty and staff. One of the oldest traditions, the **Distribution of Prizes,** began on August 4, 1822.

*Several persons present... appeared highly pleased with the pieces which the children played well, but above all with the poetry of Louise Montbrain repeated à merveille. Everyone was disappointed on finding she got no prize... the Medallion was (for the first time) given to Zelia Rousseau (who afterwards married Mr. Alexander Mouton.)* [1]

Distribution of prizes "*established in the American school an old traditional French custom of crowning the prize-winners with garlands of flowers. Usually the program for the occasion included the recitation of geography or poems in French and English.... Until only recently outsiders (even parents) were not invited to Prizes, only students, faculty and clergy (visiting) were invited. Now at Coteau all guests [are] invited to graduation....*[2]

*Distribution of prizes is a tradition that began in 1822 and continues in one form or another.*

For many years at all-school assemblies, each student was given a *Très Bien* card indicating her recent behavior: Very Good, Good, or Indifferent. Another long-standing tradition is the **awarding of Ribbons**, the first mention of which is recorded on September 6, 1830, and the first mention of students'

*Student uniforms have changed over the years, from pink to black to navy to plaid. In the 1930s, it was the middy blouse (far left) with navy skirt; 50 years later the outfits featured plaid.*

99

*Graduation in white gowns is a cherished tradition, held outdoors under the oaks, weather permitting, and a Mass is part of the ceremony.*

*When it rains on graduation day, the umbrellas come out and the ceremony is moved to the Chapel.*

voting for Ribbons was recorded on October 3, 1852.

...All the boarders wanted to rise early to make their meditation, in order to begin this beautiful day well. Father Estevan came, accompanied by some other priests. Twenty-one Blue Ribbons, as well as some green and red ones, were merited, and we can affirm that they were given according to the majority of votes of the pupils. They reacted well when they were invited to vote, giving their votes only to the pupils who had been faithful to silence. [3]

Ribbons of merit continue to be awarded at **Honors Assembly** every quarter and are voted on by students. The ribbons represent growth in one or more of the five Goals of Sacred Heart Education.

A less-loved tradition is that of *Examen* at the end of each term. Even at the end of the first school year – August 3, 1822 – there were exams. They continue today.

Perhaps not a custom, but certainly a part of daily life is the **student uniform**. Uniforms have long been required for the school day and school events unless, of course, there is a free-dress day. They have seen much variety over two centuries and identify the wearer as a student of the Academy. In the 1880s, students wore pink uniforms, but by 1889 they wore somber black. During the early years of the 1900s, a white blouse and blue skirt made up the uniform, and by the 1930s students wore a middy blouse with a navy skirt. In the second half of the 20th century, the uniform was a plaid skirt and a white oxford shirt; eventually, white or navy polo shirts were added.

In relatively recent times, saddle oxfords, ushered in by Prep School principal Sr. Maureen Little, were required, and the shoe proved so popular that some other area schools made them part of their uniforms. With the addition of the Primary School, "jumpers" for the much younger students were required.

As the 21st century approached, the style was changed to allow navy slacks and plaid knee-length shorts, as well as school logo sweat shirts. The young men at Berchmans wear white or blue button-down shirts with khaki pants and add a blue blazer for the formal uniform.

One welcome addition has been the wearing of a red sweater and red socks – but just for the senior girls, the IV Academics.

The IV Academics have another cherished tradition that is often preceded with prayers for good weather: **graduation** in Oakdale, the oak alley across the street from the school. As early as 1960, Academy graduates have gathered every year in the library to prepare for their graduation. After processing onto the gallery and through the gardens past the statue of the Sacred Heart of Jesus, the girls gather under the oaks with their families, friends, faculty, and administration for a celebration of Mass and the awarding of diplomas. In some past years, rain has altered the plans for an outdoor graduation, and when that happens the ceremony is held in the Chapel.

Another beloved tradition is *congé*, dating back to the 1800s, which was first just

Congé *is a "fun day" at the Academy, dating back to the 1800s. Held in the spring, it features food, music, games and more. Photo at right is a* congé *from the 1940s or '50s, while the picture of the band is from the 1970s.*

Traditions, Customs & Activities **103**

*Students of all ages seem to enjoy the traditional* goûter, *or snack, which is offered occasionally during the school year.*

a family "play day," often at Christmas. Later *congés* were for the students, who were often wakened by older students running through the dormitories yelling *congé*. These days, the IV Academics plan an unannounced – but highly anticipated – day of fun for the Academy and Berchmans students. A staple of the student *congé* is **goûter**, or a snack, usually a cookie or muffin accompanied by milk or juice. A special pink goûter is served on the Feast of *Mater*.

Over the years the family *congé* has grown into a much-anticipated event involving music, food, a silent auction, arts and crafts, a plant sale, and various outdoor games, sometimes even a dunking booth. It is a spring activity that combines family fun with the raising of additional funds for the continuing operation of the school.

A fairly new tradition, which started in the mid-1980s, is **Christmas at Coteau**, a shopping extravaganza fundraiser. The gym, the library, the quad, and the gallery are transformed by various vendors, who set up booths selling a variety of items including ornaments, clothing, jewelry, birdcages, artwork and books, to name just a few. Students in the Primary grades and the Academic choir entertain guests with

◀ *Held each May, the Crowning of the Blessed Mother is a solemn ceremony honoring the mother of Jesus.*

*Christmas at Coteau is a 3-day fundraising event staged at the Academy each December. The gymnasium, front gallery and library are converted to a holiday marketplace. The public at large comes to shop at the booths for jewelry, art, books, clothing, religious articles and more.*

traditional Christmas songs in the Chapel, and III and IV Academics help serve at the often sold-out luncheons prepared by various renowned Louisiana chefs.

**Feast days** continue to be celebrated. For many decades every May, selected Academy students from each grade led an all-school procession to the Lourdes grotto on the front grounds. There the student body and faculty gathered at the base of the grotto to pray and honor Mary, the Mother of God. The **May Crowning** is now done as two events, one for the Elementary School and one for the Academics. One Prep and one Academic crown the statue of Mary. They are each accompanied by an Honor Guard comprised of class representatives voted on by classmates. They carry flowers for Mary that are placed in a vase at the base of the grotto.

Another event honoring the Blessed Mother occurs annually on or near October 20: the **Crowning of *Mater Admirabilis*'** statue at the end of Memorare Hall by the staircase. The crown, placed by a senior selected by her peers, is fashioned from the seniors' class rings.

Students, especially the Academics, often stop by the statue for a prayer and a light touch on the toe of *Mater*.

*The Blessing of the Animals is held annually near the feast day of St. Francis of Assisi. At left is Sr. McDuffie, shaking hands with "Brother Dog," as St. Francis would call him.*

On or near the feast of St. Francis, parents of students bring their cats, dogs, birds and other animals for a special **Blessing of the Animals** following Mass. The quadrangle resounds with barks, meows, chirps, grunts, and sometimes even the neighs of horses.

For many decades, students have planned and participated in school-wide **Mission Carnivals**, the proceeds of which have been distributed to various Catholic charities, to the Thensted Center in Grand Coteau, and to pay the tuition of a student at the Sacred Heart school in Uganda. The Prep School Student Council organizes this event to take place at the end of October, to coincide with Halloween. Many games of skill are involved, and students are invited to showcase their creativity through participation in a Halloween costume contest.

Utilizing the talents of students, teachers traditionally have rehearsed and prepared students for **musical presentations and play productions**. The Winter and Spring Concerts fill both the chapel and the auditorium with the sound of music. The plays are highly anticipated by the Coteau family and involve both Prep and Academic students. The performances have included *Oliver, Steel Magnolias, The Wizard of Oz,* and *Aladdin,* while the Lower School has presented an annual Advent program based on the Nativity.

The **Athletic Program** at the Academy has provided avenues for leadership, healthy living and commitment, while fostering self-discipline. As a member of the Louisiana

High School Athletic Association, the school has introduced and promoted team and individual sports. Many students participate in athletics, both in team sports and in individual efforts, including basketball, volleyball, softball, tennis, soccer, swimming, equestrian arts, cross country, cheer, and track and field. Through the years, Academy teams have made numerous district and State Championship appearances, as well as having produced All-American finalists.

For years the Academy has been well-known among Network schools for its **Equestrian Program**. The large campus with its acres of fields allows ample room for practice and performance of equestrian arts. While the mid-19th century barn is still used in a limited way, the equestrian program has benefited from the construction of new barns and riding arenas. Area-wide competitions are often held on campus.

*The Equestrian Program has been a truly unique feature of the Academy for generations.*

*Many a girl has enjoyed participating in the Athletic Program over the years, whether individually or as part of a team. One such group of athletes made up this basketball team in the late 1940s.*

# Chapter 19

# The Saints of Sacred Heart

Few schools in America can claim a close association with a saint, let alone with three. But the Academy of the Sacred Heart in Grand Coteau can. Three saints, including two Religious of the Sacred Heart and one Jesuit, are closely affiliated with the Academy and have deeply impacted the life of the school.

---

 ## St. Madeleine Sophie Barat, RSCJ

### (1779-1865)

*Your example, even more than your words, will be an eloquent lesson to the world.*
— Madeleine Sophie Barat

St. Madeleine Sophie Barat, born in Joigny, France, has certainly had an impact not only on Grand Coteau but also on more than 150 Sacred Heart schools and missions worldwide.

A bright and determined child, Madeleine Sophie lived a simple life with her family. Her father, Jacques, was a respected cooper in French wine country, and her mother, Marie Madeleine, was from the Fouffé family, which could afford to gift the newlyweds with a house. She had two siblings: her brother, Louis, born March 30, 1768, and her sister, Marie-Louise Madeleine, born two years later, on August 25, 1770.

Madeleine Sophie was born on December 12, 1779, two months early, during a terrible fire that consumed several residences and stopped just three houses shy of the Barat home. Very sickly and frail, she early on displayed a bright precociousness and a great sanctity.

Fortuitously, in a time when girls were seldom educated beyond a rudimentary level, she was afforded a remarkable education. Eighteen-year-old Louis, a strict taskmaster, began teaching her when she was 7; his lessons for his little sister included mathematics, history, science, Greek, and Latin. She had a great love for books, and especially enjoyed Samuel Richardson's *Clarissa* and Cervantes' *Don Quixote*, as well as Virgil, which she read in Latin. Madeleine Sophie was receiving an education nearly unheard-of for females at that time, one most girls could only dream about. Proving that sometimes the student surpasses the teacher, she outscored Louis when he administered the same examinations that he had taken.

**St. Madeleine Sophie Barat, RSCJ**

At age 16, under pressure from Louis, she went to Paris for further independent study directed by her brother and followed a demanding curriculum of Latin, mathematics, Biblical studies, and theology.

During her years as a student she experienced the far-reaching violence and chaos of the French Revolution. She once considered becoming a Carmelite nun, but her confessor in Joigny had other plans for her, suggesting that she settle down and get married, as her sister had done.

But she was led to a different path.

At that time in early 1796, two priests, Father Léonor François de Tournély and Fr. Joseph Desiré Varin, began a new, but short-lived, religious order for men – the Fathers of the Sacred Heart – which, at the request of Pope Pius VI, later merged with the Fathers of the Faith. They realized that a Society for women should also be established. When Fr. Varin met Madeleine Sophie through his acquaintance with Louis, Fr. Varin recognized in her the qualities needed for such an order for women.

Guided by Fr. Varin, Madeleine Sophie and three companions on November 21, 1800, made their first consecration to the Sacred Heart in what would become the Society of the Sacred Heart. Her goal was to make known the love of the Heart of Jesus and to restore Christian life in post-revolutionary-war France by educating women of all classes, both rich and poor.

She was only 20.

The first convent and boarding school of the Society of the Sacred Heart, founded in 1801, was in Amiens, France, where the association increased its membership. Three years later, Mother Barat established a second convent at Grenoble, the house where Rose Philippine Duchesne was admitted to the Society in 1804. By 1815, the Society was governed by the Constitutions and Rules drawn up by Mother Barat and Father Varin, and it soon established a convent in Paris.

Besides increasing devotion to the Sacred Heart of Jesus, she endeavored to open a boarding school, or *pensionnat*, for girls at every convent she founded, where pupils would engage in various academic studies and acquire skills that would help them to run a household. She also strived to open a free school for girls from poorer families. Recognizing the power of prayer, she started the Congregation of the Children of Mary for lay women in order to further spread devotion to the Sacred Heart.

America was on the horizon, and in 1818 the foundation of the American Mission at St. Charles, in the Missouri territory, became the forerunner of many future American

*The Saints of Sacred Heart* **109**

*An elegant statue of St. Madeleine Sophie Barat can be found in St. Peter's Basilica in Vatican City.*

convents and schools. From the small beginnings in 1800, great things were happening, and it was because of Madeleine Sophie Barat's vision, faith, and persistence.

A prolific letter-writer – penning more than 14,000 lengthy letters – Mother Barat was also eloquent and pithy. Her many quotes, several of which can be found on the RSCJ website, have inspired people over 200-plus years of the Society's existence.

She often gave guidance on how to live one's life:

• *Be humble, be simple, and bring joy to others.*

• *Above all, get in the habit of thinking about God.*

• *Your example, even more than your words, will be an eloquent lesson to the world.*

• *Bear all things and give nothing to anyone else to bear.*

She had words of philosophical wisdom:

• *And what is God? Supreme happiness. That is all.*

• *Shouldn't we gratefully accept both good and bad as coming from the hand of God, for both are inclined to our advantage if we know how to profit from them.*

• *We cannot change our character, it is true, as easily as we change our clothes. It is the work of a lifetime. It is achieved with the grace of God and constant effort.*

But for educators, perhaps her best-known statement is the one often misquoted by many a harried teacher:

*For the sake of one child, I would have founded the Society.*

Many say it that way, but that isn't really what she said. It was about one former student, a Mexican named Ofelia, who was everything Sophie hoped a Sacred Heart alumna would be. Her remark was:

*"For the sake of an Ofelia, I would have founded the Society."*

It has become generalized with the use of *"one child."*

Mother Barat's charisma and capacity for developing close friendships with members of the Society, the clergy, students and friends in all walks of life enabled her to lead as Superior General of the Society of the Sacred Heart from her election on January 18, 1806, until her death on May 25, 1865. She oversaw the establishment of international schools, and at the time of her death, there were 89 houses and 3,359 Religious. Inspired by her deeply held spiritual ideals, these Religious promoted and educated thousands of girls and women in Europe, North Africa, and North and South America.

Hours after Madeleine Sophie's death, Pauline Perdrau, the artist who painted *Mater Admirabilis*, attempted a sketch of her superior and beloved mother, but admitted after three hours of trying that she was unable to do it. Therefore, a photographer was engaged to take the first and only photograph of the saintly 85-year-old woman.

Madeleine Sophie was originally buried in the cemetery at Conflans, a house of the novitiate in Charenton-le-Pont, on the eastern outskirts of Paris. But in 1893, her incorrupt body was exhumed, re-clothed, and re-interred in a tomb in the chapel of Our Lady of Dolours above the crypt where she had previously been buried.

Because religious suppression in France was widespread from 1901 to 1908, her still-incorrupt corpse was removed and taken to Jette, Belgium. On June 19, 2009, the Solemnity of the Sacred Heart, the shrine containing her preserved body was transferred to Saint François Xavier Church in Paris and placed in an ornate reliquary. The shrine features a beautiful stained-glass window representing Madeleine Sophie and is located in close proximity to the Hôtel de Biron, an early site of the Congregation, where she spent most of her life.

Declared venerable in 1905 and beatified on May 24, 1908, Madeleine Sophie Barat was canonized a saint by Pope Pius XI on May 25, 1925, with four members of the Barat family and multitudes of Sacred Heart Religious, teachers, and students in attendance.

A visitor to the Sacred Heart Basilica of Montmartre in Paris can see her portrait in a mosaic with other saints of France surrounding the dominant image of Jesus Christ. A statue of her can be found at St. Peter's Basilica in the Vatican as part of the Founder Saints Statues, which commemorate 39 founders of religious congregations. ■

#  St. Rose Philippine Duchesne, RSCJ

(1769-1852)

*You may dazzle the mind with a thousand brilliant discoveries of natural science; you may open new worlds of knowledge which were never dreamed of before; yet, if you have not developed in the soul of the pupil strong habits of virtue which will sustain her in the struggle of life, you have not educated her, but only put in her hand a powerful instrument of self-destruction.*

—Rose Philippine Duchesne

It was providential that St. Rose Philippine Duchesne was named for both the apostle Phillip and Rose of Lima, the first saint of the American continent, as she, too, would become an early saint of North America.

**St. Rose Philippine Duchesne, RSCJ**

Born into a well-respected and prosperous family in Grenoble, France, on August 29, 1769, Philippine was one of five surviving children. By necessity, she learned the many skills involved in the management of a household and in the care of small children, becoming adept at churning butter, baking bread, dipping candles and trimming their wicks, making and mending clothes, and nursing the sick. Her parents were hardworking, middle-class people who were coming into easier circumstances as France was changing for the bourgeoisie, bringing them better housing, food, and education.

Her father was Pierre-François Duchesne, who was to distinguish himself in legal, political, and social matters, becoming a political figure whom even Napoleon Bonaparte respected. He married Rose-Euphrosine Perier, the daughter of a family of high principles and success in the textile industry. She was a woman of poise, distinction, and an affectionate heart, with a fervent Catholic faith that strengthened her through the deaths of two children. She managed her large family with love and a firm hand and became the mother of a saint.

As a child, Philippine was a beautiful girl with luminous eyes and a winning smile, although small-pox disfigured her young face with scars that eventually softened and disappeared in her later life. The daughter of a large, loving family, she was trained to piety, simplicity, courtesy, consideration, obedience and self-control – traits that would define her life. A girl who was often content to be alone to contemplate and pray, she also relished others' company, particularly that of Fr. Jean-Baptiste Aubert, who had been a missionary in Louisiana and in the Illinois country. From him she heard tales of his work

# 112 *Academy of the Sacred Heart at Grand Coteau*

among the French settlers and the Native American Indians, tales that fostered in her a desire to serve as a missionary in the New World and do great things for God.

The year 1778 brought with it much tragedy for the family, as well as for the community. Philippine's older sister, Marie-Adelaide, died, leaving Philippine now the eldest child with new responsibilities. Then, on October 26-27, the Flood of Saint Crispin devastated Grenoble, leaving many citizens homeless in an area fetid with slime that covered furniture, merchandise, and food. The Duchesnes and the Periers actively worked to bring aid to those most affected by the flooding. The men transported much-needed supplies while the women prepared food and clothing for the unfortunates.

Philippine would be forever influenced by that example of generosity given by her family to those most in need, and later in life she would experience similar floods and privations along the Mississippi and rivers she did not yet know.

In 1781, in order to prepare for her First Communion, Philippine became a boarder at the Visitation Monastery of St. Marie d'en Haut, halfway up Mount Rachais near Grenoble. Here she spent a few years in formal education and studied a curriculum that included religion, arithmetic, history, French classic literature, geography, composition, and practical skills such as needlework.

After making her First Communion, on the feast of Pentecost on May 19, 1782, Philippine offered herself wholeheartedly to God. The religious life became her goal. However, this was not met with approval by her parents, who thought she was much too young to make so lasting a decision. Her father quickly withdrew her from the school. Philippine acquiesced. But she did not give up. She entered into family life and enjoyed concerts, soirees, and parties with her many cousins and friends.

She dressed in the fashion of the day with full skirts, beautiful hats, and fine gloves. She learned to dance and practiced the many difficult steps involved. She studied music and drawing and continued to develop her writing skills. But she still found her true joy in contemplating her life ahead as a religious. Even when her father entertained the idea of her marriage to a suitable young man, Philippine held fast to her vocation. She wished to be a nun.

In the spring of 1788, Philippine entreated her aunt to accompany her to the Visitation monastery. Tante Perier was the aunt who truly understood her 18-year-old niece's conviction and determination to become a nun, so she went with her to talk with Mother de Murinais about her admission to the cloister. Philippine was adamant about her vocation and she announced her decision to stay at the monastery if Mother would accept her.

Tante Perier went home alone. Despite the pleadings of her parents, Philippine was constant in her desire. She remained steadfast and did not leave with them. She had often prayed, *"Introibo ad altare Dei* – I will go unto the altar of God." [1]

Philippine became a member of the Visitation religious community as a postulant and later was given the habit and became a novice in 1788. She never made vows, which she would have done after two years, because her father would not give consent. When that community was dispersed in September of 1792, during the French Revolution, Philippine returned home, to help in taking care of those in need. She had spent four and a half years in the cloister that had become home to her, but now she was thrust into a new life.

The years 1793 to 1804 tested the resolve of the young woman. France was in the midst of a revolution and many changes of fortune affected the Duchesne-Perier families, including the murder of an uncle and the death of Philippine's mother on June 30, 1797. Philippine held her in her arms as she was dying.

For many long years, she had been longing to return to the religious life. Finally, in December of 1801, she was able to re-establish the cloister she had had to leave nine years earlier. Despite her best intentions and hard work, it was an enterprise that had an uncertain and precarious future, and by 1804 the Visitation monastery had clearly failed.

Then, on December 13, 1804, she met Madeleine Sophie Barat. It was a meeting that continues to bear fruit.

Eager to meet the religious women at the cloister of Sainte Marie, Mother Barat and her companions traveled to the convent. They had just entered a corridor when a slender figure came running toward them. Philippine prostrated herself at the feet of Mother Barat, repeating the words of a psalm: "How lovely on the mountain are the feet of those who bring the gospel of peace." [2]

"I let her do it through pure stupefaction," Mother Barat used to say, as she told of their first meeting. "I was utterly dumbfounded at the sight of such faith and humility, and I did not know what to say or do." [3]

From this meeting grew a lasting enterprise and soon Philippine became a Religious of the Sacred Heart. For 13 years she collaborated with her friend and fellow nun, acting as mistress general at the house in Grenoble. There she directed the boarding school and taught Christian doctrine and geography. One of her students, Louise de Vidaud, wrote lovingly of her teacher:

"…we were so fortunate to have her as mistress of the higher classes, we found her manner of teaching very clear and interesting, but woe to the girl who was inattentive to her explanations…. Frequently she spoke of her ardent missionary desires." [4]

She would ask the girls which one of them wanted to go with her to America to convert the Illinois Confederation, a group of Native American tribes.

Louise de Vidaud also recounted a charming account of Mother Duchesne's prayerfulness:

> An angel in adoration in the church would not have impressed us more…. Kneeling on the floor, upright and without support, hands clasped, she remained motionless for hours…. Each year she spent the entire night of Holy Thursday to Good Friday rapt in adoration before the Blessed Sacrament. Aloysia Rambaud, who often noticed her in the chapel as late as ten o'clock in the evening, and found her in the same place next morning, cut tiny bits of paper one Thursday night and dropped them on the skirt

*Academy of the Sacred Heart at Grand Coteau*

of Mother Duchesne's dress before retiring. "If she moves, the papers will tell me so." Hurrying to the chapel Friday morning to gather evidence, she found the good Mother in the same posture, the papers undisturbed, so the whole night had been spent motionless. It is easy to understand why we considered her a saint! [5]

In 1815, she was elected secretary general and moved to Paris, where she had the responsibility to establish a new motherhouse. Still she was persistent in her desire to become a missionary in America. Finally, through the mediation of Louis Barat, Madeleine Sophie Barat's brother, Philippine's desire became a possibility. A letter to Philippine from Louis arrived in 1817 telling her of a conversation he had had with Bishop William Dubourg during which the bishop had expressed his desire for Philippine to undertake missionary work in North America. The Bishop's January 14, 1817, visit with Mother Barat brought up the matter, and within a little more than a year, after much preparation and fund-raising for the venture, Philippine and four companions set sail on the *Rebecca* on March 21, 1818, from Bordeaux.

Two months later, they reached America and stayed with the Ursulines in New Orleans for a time before beginning a journey fraught with peril and illness up the Mississippi River. They were still months away from their destination – not St. Louis as expected, but the trade center of St. Charles, in the Missouri territory.

On September 14, 1818, a school opened at St. Charles, the first free school for girls west of the Mississippi. They were taught religion, reading, writing, and counting. At first the pupils were unruly and undisciplined, and Mother Duchesne devoted herself to their formation with great enthusiasm and passion. Gradually they responded to the instruction and devotion of the nuns, and a mutual respect was growing. A day school for students who could pay a nominal fee was started, and by October 1 the boarding school opened with three students. The following summer the bishop moved the school to nearby Florissant. It was more than a decade before she could re-open the school in St. Charles.

Philippine would spend the rest of her life in the New World, opening and administering schools in Missouri and Louisiana and ministering to the Potawatomie near present-day Mound City, Kansas. She finally realized her desire to be a missionary to the Indians when she was 72 years old and no longer a superior.

Now, a Jesuit school for the Potawatomie had opened in Sugar Creek, Kansas. The head of the mission asked specifically for Philippine:

"She must come; she may not be able to do much work, but she will assure success to the mission by praying for us." [6]

Frustrated by her inability to learn their language, she prayed. She prayed so much that the Potawatomie gave her the name *Quakahkanumad*, or the "woman-who-prays-always." She was able to remain in their midst for only a year before she was ordered back to St. Charles, where she lived another ten years, residing in a small room near the chapel.

Rose Philippine Duchesne died November 18, 1852, and her remains are enshrined at the Academy of the Sacred Heart in St. Charles. She was declared Venerable in 1909, beatified in 1940, and canonized by Pope John Paul II in 1988. Children of the Sacred Heart from around the world attended her canonization. Her feast is celebrated on November 18.

She had lived through the French Revolution, witnessed the rise of Napoleon, opened schools in the New World, and lived among Native American Indians when she was quite advanced in age. Surely, among the reasons for her canonization was her prayerful submission to the will of God and the decades of work she did in His name.

Visitors to the museum on the Grand Coteau campus can see the desk she used during her 1822 and 1829 visits to Coteau. Considered a Patroness of the Archdiocese of St. Louis, she has been portrayed in a Hildreth Meiere mosaic gracing an arch of the ceiling of St. Louis Basilica/Cathedral.

The Saint Philippine Duchesne Memorial Park near Mound City, Kansas, was dedicated in 1988; it is located on the grounds of the original Sugar Creek Mission. In the Mound City Catholic Church one can find beautiful stained glass windows that depict the life of Philippine. ∎

##  St. John Berchmans, S.J.

(1599-1621)

*"If I do not become a saint when I am young, I shall never become one."*
— St. John Berchmans, S.J.

Because he lived a life of piety and service to others, John Berchmans became a saint while he was young.

He was only 22 years old when he died in 1621 from Roman fever, a condition that caused inflammation of the lungs, diminishing strength, dysentery, and fever. Crowds of believers gathered after his death to mourn, and that same year the process of beatification was begun.

Born in Diest, Belgium, on March 3, 1599, to a shoemaker and his wife, he was the oldest of five children. His parents were devout and took him the day after his birth, a Sunday, to be baptized. When he was still a child, his mother suffered a long and serious illness, and John would care for her, sitting at her bedside for hours to attend to her needs. In 1615 the Jesuits opened a college only a few miles from

**St. John Berchmans, S.J.**

## 116 *Academy of the Sacred Heart at Grand Coteau*

Diest, and John was one of the first to enroll. It became clear to him at an early age that he wanted to live a religious life as a Jesuit, but his father was adamantly opposed to the idea. In fact, he threatened to withdraw all financial support if John pursued his plan.

But John persisted and entered the Jesuit novitiate on September 24, 1616. He desired to become an army chaplain, which might afford him the opportunity to be martyred on the battlefield. He pursued courses in philosophy, and a few months after his entrance into the Society of Jesus he became a student at the Roman College. There he impressed others with his holiness, his special devotion to Mary, Mother of God, and his pursuit of perfection in great and small things.

In August of 1621, his third year of studies, he was stricken with the Roman fever that would take his life. He was buried in Sant'Ignazio Church in Rome, but his heart was taken to Belgium, where it rests in a silver reliquary at the church at Louvain.

> Additional information about **John Berchmans and the Miracle of Grand Coteau**, as well as related photographs and art, can be found on pages 42-45.

His impact on the Academy of the Sacred Heart in Grand Coteau is considerable. The very ill postulant Mary Wilson was cured through his intercession on December 14, 1866. The shrine dedicated to him at the Academy is located in the same room where the miracle occurred. There are more than 20 schools and churches throughout the world named for him.

Following are excerpts from the Academy's *House Journal* describing one of the celebrations of Berchman's life:

> On November 16, 1939, the Academy of the Sacred Heart celebrated the Feast of St. John Berchmans with prayerful events that drew considerable crowds.
>
> From 2 p.m., the big chapel was filled with a crowd in prayer, waiting for the moment to go in procession to the chapel of the Saint. At 3 p.m., the procession, preceded by the Cross, set off by reciting the Joyous Mysteries of the Rosary, amplified by the microphone of R.P. [Cornelius] Thensted, along the alley of the pines and then … came near the chapel. R.P. [Sam Hill] Ray, in a short but eloquent speech, retraced the miraculous event of the healing of M. Wilson.…
>
> Next, formal blessing of the Very Holy Sacrament, given at the big chapel, but … many assistants gathered outside, for lack of space. Then after the song of "Holy God," veneration of the relic from St. John Berchmans, in his little chapel for the healthy, [and] on the lower gallery for the ill. Three urns were put near the door of the little chapel for the "needs / requests," "favors obtained" or "offerings." [Note: The initials R.P. stand for Reverend *Père*, or Reverend Father.] [7]

The account records that souvenirs, medals, and images were sold in abundance. There were estimates that the crowd numbered 1,000 people, and many were hoping for miracles. Certainly, spiritual favors were obtained through the intercession of St. John Berchmans, whom the *House Journal* describes as *"our visitor of long ago."* [8] ■

# Chapter 20

# Women of Faith and Influence

One reason why the Academy of the Sacred Heart has flourished for 200 years is the quality and devotion of the many people who have served the students and their families.

An enduring enterprise needs great leaders, and the Academy has been blessed by the leadership and service of strong, intelligent, and faith-filled persons whose mission was to further the education of young women and promote the love of the Sacred Heart of Jesus. Following are brief biographies of many of those women who served in various capacities, as Mother Superior, Assistant Superior, Mistress General, Headmistress, and teacher.

These brief profiles – some of them written by students at the Academy – represent only a few of the many hundreds of women who have graced the Academy with their presence.

Note: The profiles are presented in chronological order. The italicized years indicate the time each person spent at the Academy in Grand Coteau.

## Eugénie Audé, RSCJ

### (1792-1842)

*(1821-1825)*

Mother Eugénie Audé's name is familiar to longtime Academy students and staff because she holds the distinction of being the first Mother Superior of the Academy of the Sacred Heart at Grand Coteau.

Born May 14, 1792, in *Moûtiers-en-Tarentaise*, a town in the mountains of Savoy, Eugénie was a member of two prominent families, the Métrals and the Audés. One of four children, she was prepared for a life at court, but she chose a different path and dedicated her life to God although there was nothing in her education to draw her to a religious life. In November of 1815, she left high society and entered the novitiate of the Sacred Heart in Grenoble, France.

Displaying the leadership skills necessary for positions of responsibility, she was chosen to help found a new house in Quimper while she was still a novice. Mother Madeleine Sophie Barat, the foundress of the Society of the Sacred Heart, saw in Eugénie the gifts and spirit needed in the New World, so she was selected to be one of the missionaries to travel to America in 1818.

Mother Audé had made her vows in the Society only three years earlier, and she was able to make her final profession before embarking on the long trans-Atlantic voyage. She spent three years in Florissant, Missouri, with Mother Duchesne before being selected to found the school in Louisiana.

Her arrival in Grand Coteau in September of 1821 was much anticipated by Mrs. Charles Smith, the benefactress of the Academy. When Mother Audé finally reached her destination, she was faced with a building ill-prepared for inhabitants: no windows or doors, little furniture, and dirt floors. From this inauspicious beginning, she built a school that thrived, welcoming the first students on October 5, 1821. There she served as Mother Superior until 1825, when she moved to Convent, Louisiana, a town on the Mississippi River, to establish a second Louisiana house of the Sacred Heart that would be called St. Michael's.

Named Assistant General for America, Mother Audé returned to France in 1834 to give a report. She had planned to return to America, but remained in Europe to assist Mother Barat in administrative duties for the growing Community of the Sacred Heart.

A faithful and competent assistant, Mother Audé worked diligently even though she was stricken in 1841 with lung disease while she was Superior of the *Trinità dei Monti* in Rome. She died March 6, 1842, with Mother Barat at her side.

Of her, Mother Barat said, "…It was she who in part created and sustained those fine foundations, almost all our first houses in Louisiana." [1]

Mother Audé is buried under the altar at *Trinità dei Monti*.

## Mary Ann Aloysia Hardey, RSCJ
(1809-1886)
*(1822-1825)*

Mary Ann Hardey's association with the Academy of the Sacred Heart started when she was a small child. But what a precocious small child! And what a long life of service to the Society of the Sacred Heart she lived! She certainly is one of the Academy's most notable alumnae, and her life illustrates the ideals of Sacred Heart education and fidelity to her vocation.

In a Catholic area of Maryland, Mary Ann, the second of eight children, was born on December 8, 1809, the Feast of the Immaculate Conception, in Piscataway. Because of a whooping cough epidemic in the area, pretty, golden-haired Mary Ann was taken by her grandmother to Baltimore, where she remained for four years, until she was five. She was there on September 13, 1814, when Fort McHenry was bombarded and Francis Scott Key was inspired to write the song that would become the new nation's anthem. Soon after her return to her parents, the family moved halfway across the country to Opelousas, Louisiana, which boasted a close proximity to the new school of the Sacred Heart in Grand Coteau.

**Mother Hardey**

In 1822, the fledgling enterprise had only 14 students, who were then charged $45 per quarter tuition. Because the Hardey family was unable to pay that full price, an agreement was reached that their family slaves would do the school's laundry for a $10 reduction in tuition.

Twelve-year-old Mary Ann arrived at Grand Coteau later in the school year and discovered she needed to learn French, since most classes were taught in that language. When she graduated September 18, 1824, she was awarded the Prize of Excellence, but perhaps more importantly to her was the certain knowledge that she would become a Religious of the Sacred Heart.

She entered the Society on September 29, 1825, and since she could no longer be bothered to care for her long, beautiful hair, she simply cut it all off. On October 22, 1825, she took the habit and chose Aloysia as her new name, making her final profession on July 19, 1833. By that time she was living at St. Michael's convent near the Mississippi River, where she had been Mistress General since she was 17.

Accompanying Mother Hardey was Eliza Nebbitt, a young enslaved person. Eliza had come with

Mother Audé and Mother Hardey to the foundation of St. Michael's. Records of the time provide some information about Eliza:

Eliza, or Lisa, Nebbitt was born into slavery in Kentucky and was brought as a child to Missouri, where she was given by Bishop DuBourg to Philippine Duchesne. She lived for some years with the Sacred Heart community in Florissant, then came to Grand Coteau for a few months before moving with Eugénie Audé to the foundation at Saint Michael, where she was especially endeared to Mother Hardey. After at least two failed marriages, she returned to the convent and died there in 1889.

Mother Hardey enjoyed a long, illustrious career in teaching and administration. Many years of her life were spent in various foundations of the Society of the Sacred Heart, particularly in New York, Canada, and Cuba, and she made several trans-Atlantic trips to Europe, the first American RSCJ to attend a General Council (1842) and at 30, the youngest person in attendance. In 1844 she was charged with the responsibilities and supervision of the houses of the East and was based in New York for the next 25 years. In 1872, Aloysia Hardey was named the first American Assistant General of the Society of the Sacred Heart, and she remained in that position until her death.

After enduring the lingering effects of a heart attack for nearly ten months, Mother Aloysia Hardey died in France, on June 17, 1886. At first she was buried at the Convent at Conflans near Paris, but in the summer of 1905 her body was transported to America – her twentieth Atlantic crossing. She was reburied at Kenwood Convent of the Sacred Heart in New York.

# Carmelite Landry, RSCJ

## (1794-1852)
### *(1822-1852)*

A "Cajun" nun from Lafourche Parish, La., Carmelite Landry was born to a patriarchal family that had migrated from Canada during the infamous Acadian Exile of the mid-1700s. A good example to the young girls she knew, she was encouraged by her confessor to become a nun. After a two-year stay with the Ursulines in New Orleans, she returned to her home to seek guidance from God through prayer and contemplation.

When Mother Anna Xavier Murphy came to Louisiana in 1822, Carmelite was inspired to enter the Society of the Sacred Heart at Grand Coteau. She endured great physical hardships, as did all the nuns who helped carry water a quarter of a mile, wash the clothes, and work the fields with a plow. But nothing could weaken the vocation of this young woman who had known a life of some privilege before becoming a postulant.

Her death is recorded in the *House Journal* and describes in some detail the agonies she suffered willingly.

*Her death was the evening of a beautiful day.... She was stricken the first Sunday after Epiphany and the disease made such rapid progress that the doctor advised her to receive the Last Sacraments.... She renewed her vows, and asked pardon for the bad example she said she had given.... She died at the moment when Mother Lévèque... invoked the choir of virgins to come forth to meet her. After her death, her features, which had been entirely altered by the horrible sufferings of her agony, took on again their former serenity....* [2]

Mother Landry is buried next to Mother Anna Xavier Murphy, whom she loved dearly. They rest in the cemetery on the grounds of the Academy of the Sacred Heart in Grand Coteau.

## Anna Xavier Murphy, RSCJ
### (1793-1836)
#### (1822-1836)

So beloved in Grand Coteau was Mother Anna Xavier Murphy that baptismal records for the area show that 16 of the 49 persons baptized from 1826 to 1836 chose Xavier as their baptismal name. Mother Murphy certainly had a major influence on the community during her tenure at the Academy – and not just on baptismal names.

She is the Mother Superior whose name is associated with the iconic facade of the main building of the Academy. She had many plans for the physical and educational growth of the school and she saw some of them realized before her death in 1836. She also was responsible for reuniting several enslaved persons with their families.

Born in Ireland, Anna was educated by the Ursulines in Cork and entered the Society of the Sacred Heart in Paris. She impressed Mother Madeleine Sophie Barat for many reasons, not the least of which was her knowledge of the English language. That, coupled with her desire to serve, led to her dispatch to the New World shortly after her first profession of vows on November 6, 1821. She reached Grand Coteau March 20, 1822, and Bishop DuBourg declared that she was ready to make her final profession. She became the first RSCJ to be finally professed in the New World, on May 14, 1822.

Her work as Mother Superior was well-received by the students, families, and citizens of the surrounding area. Even Protestants were charmed by her and supported her venture at the Academy. But her poor health took a strong hold on her shortly after she arrived; she wrote of a fever, which was probably malaria. In her last year at Coteau, her last year of life, she oversaw the making of 200,000 bricks and the preparation of the lime and wood needed for planned additions to the central building.

Confined to her bed in August of 1836, she died shortly thereafter on September 6, 1836. She is buried in the Academy cemetery in Grand Coteau, next to her faithful assistant, Mother Carmelite Landry.

## Louise Dorival, RSCJ
### (1795-1832)
#### (1827-1832)

Louise Dorival advanced the mission of Sacred Heart not only by increasing the faith of those around her, but also by serving as an example of staying humble and having a strong relationship with God.

Dorival was born in Paris, France, on May 20, 1795. She worked at the Sacred Heart school in Paris until 1827. She was then assigned to the new Sacred Heart school in Grand Coteau to direct classes while serving as an assistant to Mother Superior Xavier Murphy.

After Mother Dorival's first year in Grand Coteau, Mother Xavier Murphy became sick with fever. Upon hearing this, the 37-year-old Dorival prayed to God to take the sickness from Mother Xavier and to give it to her instead. Soon after that prayer, Mother Xavier miraculously recovered, and Mother Dorival became ill with tuberculosis, known at the time as consumption. From that moment on, Dorival would not allow anyone to pray for her healing; the will of God was everything to her. She died of tuberculosis on July 11, 1832. She is buried in Grand Coteau, in the place where her true mission began. She bears the distinction of being the first person buried in the community cemetery.

Mother Dorival will be remembered for her great example of humility and for her eternal trust in God's will. Her colleagues remembered her as a woman of faith, grace, prudence, amiability, and tender devotion to the Blessed Virgin Mary.

Source: Mother Xavier Superior's letter, July 12, 1832, Grand Coteau

*House Journal,* 1821-1884, Aug. to Dec., 1827, and July to October, 1832

— *Ana Castille,* Class of 2023

# Maria Cutts, RSCJ

## (1811-1854)

### *(1836-1854)*

Witnessing Mother Maria Cutts' fifth operation for cancer, Fr. Rocofort, SJ, declared, "*If Mother Cutts were my superior, I would go through fire to carry out her orders, for assuredly she is a saint, and a great saint.*" [3] Mother Cutts certainly was thought to be a saint by the Jesuits, the Society of the Sacred Heart, the Grand Coteau community, the parents, and particularly the students of the Academy.

Having arrived at the school in 1836 to serve as Mistress General of the *pensionnat*, or boarding school, she became the Mother Superior in 1841 after the departure of Mother Bazire. However, she did double duty, serving as the school's Superior and in 1844, working as the Visitatrice of the Western houses: St. Louis, St. Charles, St. Ferdinand, St. Michael, and Sugar Creek. This involved quite a lot of traveling, often in arduous and dangerous conditions.

During her many years of service in Grand Coteau, she oversaw the care of students, orphans, and novices, as well as the members of her Community. She endeavored to teach English to Native Americans desirous of learning about God. She motivated them to learn the language – so difficult for many – with a reward of a miraculous medal. During times of outbreaks of measles, bilious fever, scarlet fever, and yellow fever, she was sometimes the only one able to nurse. However, most of her years at Coteau were marked by her own illnesses, fevers, asthma, and finally cancer.

In 1825, the RSCJ novitiate that had been opened in 1821 in Grand Coteau was moved to St. Michael's, in St. James Parish. Years later, Mother Cutts facilitated the return of the novitiate to Grand Coteau, and seven novices and three postulants arrived in 1848. By 1849 there were 16 choir religious and one sister novice. And the school saw growth with 116 boarders and the need to provide housing for eight day-students.

The quality of their academic accomplishment and the good behavior of the students inspired Mother Cutts to compliment the pupils. She said, "*...it was only right that children so dear to the Sacred Heart in Louisiana should be the model of all other schools in the state.*" [4] She often rewarded them with entertainments such as "magic lantern" shows and *congés*.

Mother Maria Cutts died October 24, 1854, of cancer after undergoing five operations to remove the tumor that grew on her arm and on one side of her chest. She is buried in the Sacred Heart cemetery at Grand Coteau.

# Julie Bazire, RSCJ

## (1806-1883)

### *(1837-1840)*

Julie Bazire was born in LaMarche, France, in 1806, during the Napoleonic era. After entering the Society in 1825, she came to the United States in 1829, where she made her final profession a year later in St. Louis.

She served as Reverend Mother in Louisiana, first in Lafourche, then at St. Michael's. In March of 1837, she was selected to be the Mother Superior at Grand Coteau after the death of Mother Xavier Murphy.

Bazire was the Mother Superior who welcomed Jesuit priests to the heart of Louisiana. It was her gift of the 200,000 bricks that had been intended for the new Academy chapel that enabled the Jesuits to establish their college in Grand Coteau. She also gifted them with three trees – peach, fig, and pecan – for their garden.

Mother Bazire had a compassionate, yet authoritative manner with her pupils. When a penniless mother of five lay dying, the devout Catholic implored Mother Bazire to care for her children. Mother Bazire willingly and graciously took under her wing and protection the four orphaned daughters while the Jesuits cared for the teenaged son.

But when three pupils, as a lark, ran away during evening recreation, Mother Bazire was firm with them upon their return. They got only as far as a neighbor's house before the neighbor reported them to the school. Mother Bazire kept them under strict surveillance for several days, and they quickly asked her pardon.

In the last year of her tenure as Mother Superior, Mother Bazire oversaw the construction of two brick buildings, one a bathhouse and the other a *buanderie*, or laundry. Under her direction, the enrollment of the school grew to 109 pupils, and she obtained a new organ for the chapel. She also oversaw the beginning of an orphanage on the grounds.

After relocating to St. Louis, she moved back to France in 1843; in 1847 she returned to America, until 1850. She died in France February 22, 1883.

## Mary Elizabeth Moran, RSCJ
### (1836-1905)
*(1853-1879)*

Mary Elizabeth Moran was a child of New Orleans, where she lost her father when she was eight years old and her mother six years later. Born March 13, 1836, she became a boarder at the Academy of the Sacred Heart in Grand Coteau in late November 1850. She was an exemplary student and was awarded the Prize of Excellence on August 16, 1853, a prize awarded only when there is a student worthy of the honor.

She was to excel in various areas of service to God's people after she joined the Society of the Sacred Heart as a postulant on October 17, 1853.

During her early years in the Society she suffered with yellow fever and witnessed the deaths of many who succumbed to measles, fever, and other illnesses. She took the habit on March 3, 1854, and made first vows December 27, 1855. Her final profession came during the Civil War, on August 19, 1862, a turbulent time in the school's history.

On March 3, 1864, she confronted soldiers at the Academy. The incident is related in *Southward Ho!*

"...they (Mary and a companion on night duty) heard a shout, 'Halt, or I will kill you!' All those living on the property converged on the spot, crying to be sheltered as armed men came into the courtyard and struck Mother Jouve on the cheek. Mary moved in front, and with great dignity said, 'Are you men that would frighten to death young and innocent children?' The leader said, 'Are there

**Mother Moran**

*children here?' 'Yes,' she continued, 'and they are confided to us by their parents to whom we must answer.' With this, the leader took the intruders away."* [5]

For 19 years at Grand Coteau, Mother Moran was at various times a teacher, treasurer, assistant, and Mistress General. She was one of the nurses for Mary Wilson, who was miraculously cured through the intercession of Blessed John Berchmans. Mother Moran's testimony was part of the Vatican's canonization process for Berchmans.

Among her many duties was the education of newly freed persons of color in the area, and in 1875 she helped found a school for the girls in Grand Coteau.

In 1876 Mother Moran became vicar for the Louisiana houses, and at age 40 she began an extraordinary time when she oversaw the foundation of seven houses in four countries. In 1879 she left Grand Coteau, where she had lived for 29 years, and moved to St. Michael's, a move marking the beginning of many trips in America and abroad.

Her final residence was in Belgium, John Berchmans' native land, where she died on August 9, 1905, and where she is buried.

## Victoria Pizarro Martinez

(1815-1884)

*(1854-81, 1883-84)*

Even as a child, Victoria Pizarro Martinez exhibited a gift for spirituality, as was observed by her teachers at Ursuline Academy in New Orleans, the city of her birth in 1815. She could be found joyfully teaching the catechism to the domestic help and to the poor.

The daughter of the Spanish consul in New Orleans, she could have had a life of prominence and privilege in society. However, she found her life's work as a Religious of the Sacred Heart, perhaps as a result of her years at Sacred Heart Convent in St. Michael's, Louisiana. Despite her father's initial strong objections to her decision, she finally received permission to enter the Society in November of 1833, a day she described as "a feast of my heart." [6]

Taking her final vows at St. Michael's, she remained there until she came to Grand Coteau in 1854 to assist Mother Louisa Lévèque with her students. Within a year's time, she became assistant to the Superior, Mother Amélie Jouve, and served in assorted jobs including sacristan. By 1855, she was Mistress of Novices, a job in which she became noted for her kindliness, firmness, and discretion with the novices.

Her role at the convent took on more responsibility when she became Superior *per interim*, when Mother Jouve journeyed to France in 1864. That interim lasted ten years, so she served as Superior, Mistress of Novices, and sacristan.

As the Superior who witnessed Mary Wilson's miraculous cure in 1866, she was instrumental in converting the infirmary where Mary was healed into the shrine honoring John Berchmans. Mother Martinez quietly took on the role as assistant to Mother Mary Elizabeth Moran when the latter became the new Superior in 1874.

After 27 years at Grand Coteau, Mother Martinez was called to New Orleans to be assistant to the Superior at the Sacred Heart school there. She was there for only two years when her failing health necessitated her to return to Grand Coteau, where she died a year later, in December of 1884. She was 69, having devoted most of her life in service to the people of God. She is buried at Grand Coteau in the school's cemetery.

**Mother Jouve**

## Marguerite-Amélie Jouve, RSCJ

(1799-1880)

*(1855-64)*

Marguerite-Amélie Jouve was born May 21, 1799, in Lyons, France, the daughter of Jean-Joseph Jouve and Charlotte-Euphrosine Duchesne, who interestingly enough was the sister of St. Rose Philippine Duchesne.

As the niece of a well-known and important religious figure, it was almost destiny for Amélie to become a Religious of the Sacred Heart herself.

Amélie's younger sister, Euphrosine, also became an RSCJ and took on the name Aloysia. Sadly, Euphrosine died at the age of 25, and in her memory Amélie adopted her name. Now named Aloysia, she entered the Society of the Sacred

Heart and made her first vows in 1823 in Paris, and her final vows a few years later.

In her later life, Mother Jouve traveled to North America in 1847, spending two weeks with her Aunt Philippine in St. Charles on her way to Montreal, Canada. She later arrived in Grand Coteau, in 1855, remaining there until 1864, a time when the Civil War was impacting life throughout the South.

Mother Jouve served as Mother Superior at the Academy from 1860 to 1863, during most of the Civil War. She played an important role in keeping the school open. Because Union General Nathaniel Banks had a daughter who went to a Sacred Heart sister school in New York, Mother Jouve asked General Banks to protect the students. His decision to do so allowed the school to remain open during the war. Without Mother Jouve's intercession, the situation could have turned out differently and the Academy most likely would have closed during the war.

Mother Amélie Jouve, an important figure in the Academy's history, traveled to France in 1864 to attend a meeting and remained in France until her death in 1880, in Orleans, France, where she is buried.

— *Caroline Corley*, Class of 2023

Works Cited:
*House Journal 1821-1884* pp. 154-160, 162, 167-169, 217-218, 244, and 247.

Sr. Carolyn Osiek, email of Feb. 10, 2020

## Emma Marie Louise Chaudet, RSCJ

### (1844-1920)

#### *(1856, 1884-88, 1892-96)*

Born in St. Landry Parish, Louisiana, on June 30, 1844, Emma Marie Louise Chaudet became a student at the Academy of the Sacred Heart when she was eleven years old. She recorded about that day when she enrolled: "*On the great day of May 8, 1856, I made the determination to give myself completely to Jesus…*" [7]

Her family soon moved to New Orleans, where her father engaged a private tutor for her. By 1863, she had written to Mother Anna Shannon, the Superior at St. Michael's, that she wished to enter the Society of the Sacred Heart. Travel at this time in the midst of the Civil War was difficult, but she safely arrived at St. Michael's and was accepted as a postulant. Three months later, she journeyed to Grand Coteau, despite the challenges of traveling during wartime.

Received by Mother Amélie Jouve and making her novitiate with Mother Victoria Martinez, Emma began her apostolic life after making her first vows in December of 1865. That life took her first to Natchitoches, Louisiana, where she made her final profession and worked in a variety of positions in the Sacred Heart school; then to Selma, Alabama, to help found a mission; then to Paris, France. Later, she returned to Grand Coteau as mistress of novices. During her many years at Coteau, she served as Superior and mistress of novices until the novitiate closed in 1896. She died in 1920 at St. Michael's and is buried there.

## Mary Wilson, RSCJ

### (1846-67)

#### *(1866-67)*

Mary Wilson, a woman born with a desire to serve, helped in the making of a saint. Born in New London, Canada, on September 20, 1846, Mary spent 16 years of her life in New London as a Presbyterian before moving to St Louis, Missouri. She soon became acquainted with many Catholics, and their unwavering faith led her to convert to Catholicism, officially on May 2, 1862, a decision that led to Mary being disowned by her own family.

However, Mary's faith was her real source of wisdom, and nearly four years after her conversion she was accepted to the novitiate of the Sacred Heart as a postulant, but she also suffered many physical ailments. The humid climate of the South was considered to be a cure in those days, so Mary journeyed to the novitiate in south Louisiana, arriving in Grand Coteau on September 20, 1866.

However, Mary's health grew worse; she was experiencing pain in her side and nausea, and she was unable to drink water. She was admitted into the convent's infirmary, and Mother Martinez suggested that she return home because the so-called healing climate wasn't working for her. Mary's doctor, however, said that she was not to be moved. Mary later reflected on the experience:

"Hearing this, I thought I had to return home, but God in his infinite wisdom did not permit it."

On December 6, 1866, Mother Martinez gave Mary a picture of Blessed John Berchmans and told her that the community would be praying a novena to him later that night. On the 10th, Mary received the Last Rites. Everyone, including the doctors, believed she was on her deathbed. That evening, Mary was alone in the infirmary when she heard a voice. Unable to open her eyes, she listened.

"Open your mouth," the voice said, and she did so as well as she could.

"I felt someone, as it were, put their finger on my tongue, and immediately, I was relieved," she recalled later.

Mary described seeing a man standing at her bedside and holding a cup, and his shape was covered by light.

"Is it Blessed Berchmans?" she asked.

"Yes, I come by the order of God; your sufferings are over, fear not. Sister, you will get the desired habit. Be faithful. Have confidence. Fear not," he replied.

Miraculously cured of the fatal illness, Mary Wilson lived the remainder of her life devoted to God and His wisdom. On December 17, 1866, Mary Wilson received the holy habit of the Sacred Heart. She died on August 17, 1867, and is buried in the Sacred Heart cemetery in Grand Coteau.

Two years after Mary's experience with the healing apparition of John Berchmans, Blessed Berchmans was canonized in Rome as a saint.

Source: "The Miracle at Grand Coteau" by Rev. C. J. McNaspy, Associate Editor of *America* and *The Catholic Mind*

— *Lauren Wiltz,* Class of 2024

**Mother Tommasini**

# Maria Stanislas Tommasini, RSCJ

(1827-1913)

*(1881-83)*

Maria Stanislas Tommasini gave 65 years of service to the Society of the Sacred Heart in America, some of it in Grand Coteau. She was born in the Duchy of Parma in northern Italy in 1827 to a simple, hard-working family. A happy child with a great love for singing and dancing, she was filled with joy.

She entered the Society in 1845 in Pinerol, Italy, and came to America in 1848, living first in Manhattanville, New York, for 23 years.

In 1870 she became the superior in Havana, and then in New York City in 1873. Prior to her arrival in Grand Coteau, in 1881, she had been superior vicar of Canada. How different Grand Coteau must have seemed to her, the international traveler and missionary. She describes her arrival:

"*Finally my star stood over Grand Coteau. At the primitive station called Sunset I found a carriage that would have satisfied Mother Duchesne. It was the convent carriage drawn by a horse....*" [8]

She served as superior and mistress of novices,

and she also gave instruction in three languages – French, Spanish, and English – so that she would be understood by all.

From Louisiana she went to Mexico, where she was to live for 13 years. Finally she retired to the Sacred Heart Community in Kenwood, New York, and died September 18, 1913. She is buried at Kenwood.

## Claire Saizan, RSCJ
### (1910-2011)
*(1938-40, 1944-45, 1947-56, 1977-2002)*

*"An educator is a mystic driven by love to share her knowledge with others."*
— Claire Saizan

Sister Claire Saizan, born in New Orleans on January 1, 1910, attended Loyola University, where she earned a bachelor's degree in 1930 and a master's in 1932, both in English. Sister Saizan taught at several Sacred Heart schools, including the Academy of the Sacred Heart in New Orleans, Villa Duchesne in St. Louis, Maryville University in St. Louis, and Academy of the Sacred Heart in Cincinnati. Her longest service was the 36 years she spent at the Academy in Grand Coteau.

At the Academy, Sister Saizan was the director of the boarding school, the *maîtresse générale du pensionnat*, from 1951 to 1956, but she was always the teacher, teaching French, math, history, Latin, and English, and moderating the school's Quiz Bowl team. She was known as "a hard teacher," especially in French, but her reputation as a Quiz Bowl moderator was even more formidable. Although students sometimes feared Sister Saizan and the intimidating cane she often banged on the floor to capture students' attention, she inspired students to reach great intellectual heights. Upon her retirement from teaching in 2002, she was appropriately presented with a new cane fashioned with wood from one of the school's historic buildings.

Sister Saizan's reputation for being a challenging, strong educator who demanded much of her students has secured her legacy at Grand Coteau,

**Sister Saizan**

where the Goal II Prize for a deep respect for intellectual values bears her name. During her time at the Academy in Grand Coteau, Sister Saizan demonstrated her great faithfulness to God through her commitment to education; she was incredibly selfless when it came to her students' needs.

Sister Claire Saizan died on February 16, 2011, at Oakwood, the Society of the Sacred Heart's retirement center in Atherton, California. She is buried in the Academy cemetery in Grand Coteau.

Sources: https://rscj.org/ ; Cynthia Thompson, '88, 10-28-19

— *Hannah Cheeran,* Class of 2023

## Carmen Smith, RSCJ
### (1920-2003)
*(1945-46, 1950-52, 1960-63, 1969-76, 1983-91, 1993-97)*

The mission of the Academy of the Sacred Heart focuses not only on educating a child academically, but also nurturing the whole child toward a deep faith in God. Sr. Carmen Margaret Smith exemplified this philosophy throughout the period in which she taught at the Academy. Born in Thibodaux, Louisiana, on August 15, 1920, she joined the Religious of the Sacred Heart at the age

**Sister Smith**

of 21. She began teaching adolescent girls across the country before coming to Grand Coteau in 1945. At the Academy, Sr. Smith taught world religions, English, and Latin. Although she taught at other Sacred Heart schools, such as Duchesne, Stone Ridge, and St. Louis, she spent most of her life in Grand Coteau.

Sr. Smith not only cultivated in her students a deep understanding of literature, but she also spent time outside of class with her students getting to know them personally and encouraging them to expand their horizons. One of her former students, Elia Caire, remembers fondly her time with Sr. Smith.

"We would sit on that sweet front porch and discuss all things literature while we sipped ice cold water with fresh lemon squeezed into it," Caire recalled.

Sister always inspired her students to write, and one way she accomplished this was with the help of the famous Louisiana author, Walker Percy. Caire remembers a class period that involved sitting with Sr. Smith and Mr. Percy under a tree in the front gardens and listening to him tell stories.

When Sr. Smith taught upper school English, she would assign a project every year to help the students grow in their poetry skills. Though some of her students said they weren't the best at poetry, Sr. Smith would inspire them to keep going and learn more.

Sr. Smith had a deep love for writing devotions and poems. In her poem, "Between the Daylight and the Dark," she reflects on the Passion of Christ and how He brings light into everyone's life. Just like Christ, Sr. Smith brought light into the lives of her students through her passion for Sacred Heart education. In her devotion to Saint Philippine, Sr. Smith wrote that the saint "ran lightly as a girl to the God of [joy]."

Sr. Smith inspired her students at the Academy to pursue the joy of God's love through literature, and she created for her students an environment that encouraged continuous learning and personal growth.

She died July 8, 2003, at Oakwood, the RSCJ retirement home in Atherton, California, and is buried there.

—*Ella Yerger and Mary Grace Thompson,* Class of 2023

Sources: rscj.com website 11-03-19; Elia Caire, ASH Alumna, 10-28-19; Linzee Lagrange, ASH Alumna, 10-28-19; Carolyn Osiek, RSCJ, Archivist, Society of the Sacred Heart, 10-29-19; Cynthia Thompson, Class of 1988, 10-28-19 .

## Antonia Plauche, RSCJ
### (1904-2002)
*(1945-60, 1965-69, 1976-90)*

Sister Antonia Plauche, also known as Mother Plauche or Sister Tony, was a religious sister, a Sacred Heart alumna, and a beloved member of the Academy of the Sacred Heart Community in Grand Coteau. She was born in Marksville, Louisiana, on June 12, 1904, and attended high school and college at the Academy in Grand Coteau from 1920 to 1926.

Not long after graduation, she made her final vows and became a nun in 1935, after which she worked as an elementary school teacher in New Orleans and St. Louis.

From 1945 to 1960, Sr. Plauche served as Treasurer and Assistant Superior at the Academy in Grand Coteau, before working at Duchesne in Houston. She returned to Grand Coteau in 1961

**Sister Plauche**

**Sister Mouton**

and served first as Assistant Superior and then Superior until 1969. Returning in 1976, she worked at various odd jobs until 1990.

During Sr. Plauche's time at Coteau, she often hosted boarders in her family home during the holidays if they could not travel to their homes. At the Academy, Sister Plauche's kind-hearted generosity left a footprint on the school's community because she was dearly loved by all. On November 22, 2002, she passed away and is buried in Atherton, California.

Source: Carolyn Osiek, RSCJ, Provincial Archivist, Society of the Sacred Heart, December 3, 2019

— *Lillian Cain,* Class of 2022

## Carolyn Mouton, RSCJ

(1928-   )

*(1955-65, 1978-85)*

Carolyn Mouton bears a name well-known and respected in Acadiana's religious circles. Her brother was the late Monsignor Richard Mouton and her aunt is Sr. Odéide Mouton, RSCJ. In fact, Carolyn is one of several Mouton women who entered the Society of the Sacred Heart!

Born in Lafayette, Louisiana, in 1928, she was educated locally. She graduated from the Sacred Heart College at Grand Coteau in 1948 and entered the Society in 1950. After making her first vows in 1953 at Kenwood in Albany, N.Y., she eventually came back to Louisiana in 1955 and taught English and French until 1958 at the Academy in Grand Coteau. After making her final profession in Rome in 1959, she returned to the Academy as its Mistress General, or Headmistress, serving in that position until 1965. She returned in 1978 and did pastoral work in the area until 1985.

She is remembered by students as being a delightful person blessed with excellent "people skills" – skills that she used often to help students who presented both academic and behavioral difficulties. As headmistress, she would conduct weekly politeness classes for the entire Prep School body. They would learn etiquette, including how to write thank-you notes, how to properly set a table, how to sit gracefully, and even how to eat a banana with a spoon.

She retired in 2006 and moved to Oakwood Retirement Center in Atherton, California.

## Anita Villere, RSCJ

(1919-2012)

*(1956-60, 1965-67, 1968-70)*

Sr. Anita Villere, better known as "Nita," was a nun noted for her Southern hospitality and artistic talent.

Born September 6, 1919, in New Orleans,

Women of Faith and Influence  **129**

**Sister Villere**

Louisiana, Nita was one of seven children – three boys and four girls, all educated in Catholic schools. Following graduation from the Convent of the Sacred Heart, "The Rosary," in New Orleans, Nita attended Maryville College in St. Louis, Missouri, on a scholarship. After her senior year at Maryville, she entered the Society of the Sacred Heart at Kenwood in Albany, N.Y., in 1941. On February 11, 1942, Nita pronounced her first vows and was assigned to the Academy of the Sacred Heart in Grand Coteau. On July 30, 1949, she made her final vows in Rome, and from then on she worked at various Sacred Heart institutions.

Sister Villere served as Headmistress at the City House in St. Louis, as well as at several Sacred Heart schools. From 1956 to 1960 and from 1965 to 1967 she was Mistress General in Grand Coteau, and in 1968 she assumed the responsibilities of Headmistress, until 1970.

From Grand Coteau, she went to Villa Duchesne in St. Louis to be a counselor. In 1971, she spent a year in the Apostolic Religious Community program in Rome. She then became principal at the Rosary, her *alma mater*, in 1976. At age 61, Anita was employed by the Archdiocese of New Orleans as the Director of Social Services at Our Lady of Lourdes Parish Center, where she ministered to older adults.

In 1995, Sr. Villere was invited to be part of the pastoral care team at the RSCJ retirement center in Atherton, California. In addition to her formal duties, she took the initiative to start teaching art classes to residents. She held regular exhibits of her students' artwork. They also provided landscapes and other drawings that were used on greeting cards. After becoming a resident herself in 2006, she continued art classes and pastoral care.

In September of 2012, Sr. Villere fell quite ill, and accepted her diagnosis of acute leukemia with the same grace and trust in God as she had lived all her life. She died on September 19, 2012, shortly after receiving the diagnosis. She is buried at Oakwood.

— *Sarah Roth,* Class of 2023

*Source: Sr. Anita Villere,* https://drive.google.com, 1/30/2020

## Rita Karam, RSCJ
(1929-1996)
*(1963-73)*

Sister Rita Karam experienced an incredibly full life as a Religious of the Sacred Heart. She was born in Kinder, in southwest Louisiana, April 13, 1929, the only daughter of Tom and Bonnie Karam. She graduated from Southwestern Louisiana Institute at Lafayette.

**Sister Karam**

She first encountered the Religious of the Sacred Heart while teaching at the Academy at Grand Coteau. It was there that she decided to become an RSCJ. After entering the Society on September 7, 1952, she received the habit Easter Wednesday 1953. She made her first vows two years later and took her final vows on February 4,

1961. After teaching at Duchesne Academy of the Sacred Heart in Houston, Sr. Karam moved back to Grand Coteau to become its principal in the fall of 1963, then served as Headmistress from 1967 to 1973.

After years of service, Sister Karam moved from ASH-Coteau to St. Louis, where she became the Mother Provincial of the Southern Province, serving from 1973 to 1982. Her term was extended to eight years – the usual term being six years – during the time that the Society was establishing a single United States Province.

From 1982 to 1988, she was a member of the General Council and resided in Rome. During her six years in Rome she traveled to 27 countries with the General Council and oversaw many activities in Rome. One of her last and greatest missions as a member of the Council was coordinating the preparations for the canonization of Philippine Duchesne in 1988; during that process, she met Pope John Paul II.

Shortly after that, Sr. Karam moved back to Louisiana to work at "the Rosary" in New Orleans, which she did until her death November 14, 1996. To memorialize and pay tribute to her for her service to the school, the Rosary instituted the *Sister Rita Karam Award for Outstanding Service to the Wider Community.*

She is buried in the cemetery at the Academy of the Sacred Heart in Grand Coteau.

Source: Christina Cain, Class of 1990, Relative of Sr. Karam, interview 12-2-19

— *Maggie Hamontree*, Class of 2022

## Barbara Moreau, RSCJ
### (1938-2019)
*(1967-71, 1978-92, 2004-10, 2013-19)*

Sister Barbara Ann Moreau embodied the spirit of the Sacred Heart mission from the time she first set foot in Grand Coteau in 1960 to her final days there in 2019.

Sr. Moreau was born on June 10, 1938, in New Orleans, to John Herbert Moreau Sr. and Una Bernadette Lalonde. Even before her first vows as an RSCJ, Sister Moreau was known as a woman

**Sister Moreau**

of service, self-sacrifice, and faithfulness. She took her first vows at Kenwood in Albany, New York, and professed her final vows as an RSCJ in Grand Coteau, where she had first encountered the religious order when she worked there as a physical education teacher several years earlier. In her early life, Sr. Moreau attended public school, often referring to herself as a "public school person." Indeed, by caring for others, she did minister to the public and taught her private school students to do likewise.

As an RSCJ, Sr. Moreau worked in administration at several Sacred Heart schools, including those in St. Louis, Missouri; St. Charles, Missouri; and Grand Coteau. She was the Dean at the Sacred Heart schools in Saint Charles and Grand Coteau, but she is best remembered for her 14 years as the Boarding School Director at Grand Coteau. Sr. Moreau lovingly cared for the boarders and formed special lasting bonds with the students. In many ways, the boarders realized the mother figure she presented in their lives and how they were deeply affected by it. When the students were in pain, she suffered with them.

Although she was gentle and caring, Sr. Moreau was also a force to be reckoned with. Many boarding students remember her as being strict, but they also appreciate how well Sr. Moreau nurtured in them the foundations of the Sacred Heart.

After her service in the Boarding School at

Grand Coteau, Sister Moreau spent time doing other educational and hospitality services for the Society of the Sacred Heart. In the final years of her life, she returned to Grand Coteau, using her expansive knowledge of the history of the school to give tours of the Shrine of Saint John Berchmans and the Academy's museum. Her mission was to preserve the history and spirit of the place she loved so much.

Sr. Moreau was a true servant of God. By her faithfulness, generosity, and love of others, she helped shape Grand Coteau's Sacred Heart community into what it is today, a community rooted in God.

After 54 years of service as an RSCJ, Sr. Moreau died in Grand Coteau on July 27, 2019, and her remains are interred in the place she lovingly served as a devoted child of the Sacred Heart.

Sources:
– https://www.rscj.org/about/memoriam/barbara-moreau-rscj 10-28-19
– Paula Moreau Chachere (Sr. Moreau's sister) - interview 11-4-19
– https://backroadplanet.com/cultural-spiritual-encounters-st-landry-parish-louisiana/10-28-19

— *Megan Hubbell*, Class of 2023

## Rose Guidroz, RSCJ
(1919-2013)

*(1968-94)*

Sister Rose Guidroz developed a reputation as the sweetest lady on campus and earned the nickname "Sister Fudge" because of the candy, especially the fudge, she routinely made for the students of the Academy.

Rose Guidroz, born March 21, 1919, with her twin sister, Anna, in Franklin, Louisiana, served at the Academy of the Sacred Heart in Grand Coteau from 1968 to 1994. She left the classroom at the age of 75 when her hearing loss became more pronounced. Then she had more time for making the candy for which she is remembered.

She dedicated her life to filling the campus with a love for Christ and helping students develop into faith-filled young ladies. She was a strong example

**Sister Guidroz**

of community service within the town of Grand Coteau, where she tutored at the Thensted Center.

Religious of the Sacred Heart are dedicated to spreading God's love in the world, and they achieve this in large part through the education of students in Sacred Heart schools. Such was the case with Sr. Rose Guidroz, who taught biology to the Upper School at the Academy.

Even after she was no longer teaching, she remained on campus making and selling her delectable fudge – then donating the proceeds to charity. She used her culinary skills as her primary way of serving and ministering; she did not make candy for the sake of making candy, but as a means of serving others, which was what she loved to do most.

"I love to do something for other people. I consider it my ministry," she once explained.

Sr. Guidroz died on February 25, 2013, at the RSCJ retirement home in Atherton, California, and is buried in the Academy's cemetery in Grand Coteau.

Sources:
– "Rose Guidroz, RSCJ." *Rose Guidroz, RSCJ | RSCJ.org*, 4 Oct. 2017, rscj.org/about/memoriam/rose-guidroz-rscj.
– Toner, Paula. "Heart- A Journal of the Society of the Sacred Heart." *Society of the Sacred Heart*, 2011, rscj.org

— *Isabel Landry*, Class of 2023

**Sister Jenkins**

## Mary Louise "Mamie" Jenkins, RSCJ
(1924-2019)
*(1971-78, 1980-83)*

A much-loved personality fondly remembered by Academy students from the 1970s and early '80s is Mary Louise Jenkins, RSCJ.

Born December 17, 1924, in Bronx, New York, "Mamie" was one of ten children. Her father, originally from the South, was a professional singer, so the children grew up with music, either singing or playing an instrument. Mamie did both beautifully.

Because she was a non-Catholic, an exception had to be made for her to attend Manhattanville College of the Sacred Heart, where she had been awarded a music scholarship. A gifted musician, she had received other scholarships but chose Manhattanville because it was within walking distance of her home. While taking classes to earn her degree, she and her music teacher also gave concerts throughout the United States.

After converting to Catholicism and knowing that she wanted to be a nun, she began the process of becoming a Religious of the Sacred Heart during her senior year. The first African-American student to attend the school, in 1946 she became its first African-American graduate and later the first African-American RSCJ. In 1951 she pronounced her first vows, and on July 30, 1956, she made her final profession in Rome.

She taught in various Sacred Heart schools in the East and the Midwest before coming to Grand Coteau, where she taught Prep School classes from 1971 until 1978. She returned to Coteau in 1980 for another three years. In addition to teaching, she also entertained students and faculty with her guitar and songs during morning assemblies and *goûters*.

A former Prep student, Sarah Maroney, knew Sr. Jenkins well and had this to say about her:

"[She was] one who graced my presence at the Academy…. She exuded the Holy Spirit with a smile of joy coupled with singing while strumming her guitar."

Sr. Jenkins was a member of several national music and social-awareness organizations, including the National Catholic Conference for Racial Justice. In 2008, she retired to Oakwood RSCJ retirement community in Atherton, California, where she brought joy to others with her music and zest for life.

She spent the morning of her death, October 2, 2019, singing before going peacefully to God. She is buried at Oakwood.

## Mathilde "Mac" McDuffie, RSCJ
(1926-2016)
*(1972-2010)*

Sr. Mathilde "Mac" McDuffie's tenure from 1972 to 2010 at the Academy of the Sacred Heart in Grand Coteau is one of the longest served there by an RSCJ. She emerged as one of the best-known and most-loved personalities ever at the Academy.

In addition to her strong relationships with her students and the faculty, she cultivated enduring bonds with several of the area residents, some of whom would help her pick pecans or care for the many Academy animals that she loved and fed.

A Midwesterner, born in Cincinnati, Ohio, on

*Women of Faith and Influence* **133**

**Sister McDuffie**

May 14, 1926, she entered the Society of the Sacred Heart October 30, 1948, despite initial objections from her parents. When they saw how happy and how determined she was to become a religious sister, they acquiesced and later took great pride in her choice. She made her first vows in 1951 and her final profession in Rome in 1957. Before coming to Grand Coteau, she had worked in various Sacred Heart schools, including the new Woodlands Academy in Lake Forest, Illinois, where she was a founding faculty member.

Mac was a dedicated teacher who loved and inspired children to be their best. She also had an abiding love for animals and nature. In fact, she became known as "the St. Francis of Grand Coteau."

Sr. McDuffie began her work at ASH in 1972 as the Director of the Boarding School, and after eight years in that role she began teaching English and religion until her retirement in 2010. She brought out the best in her students and they enjoyed her fun-loving nature and her gentleness. They also relished being allowed to help her care for the many animals on campus, some of which were abandoned by locals who knew they would be taken care of by Sr. Mac.

On the Academy's large rural campus, she had room for a multitude of animals, establishing her "Animal Kingdom" behind the school. There she cared for birds, rabbits, cats, dogs, and even a pot-bellied pig named Blossom. Two of her dogs, Sean and Coteau, would sometimes accompany her to her classroom, where they stayed quietly under her desk during classtime.

The Academy also benefitted from her horticultural skills and was rarely at a loss for flowers to adorn the chapel altar and *Mater's* statue. A member of the National Rose Society, Sr. McDuffie was renowned for her large variety of rose bushes – more than 40 different kinds. She was a familiar figure in her straw hat and gloves tending to the gardens near the Bishop's Cottage.

In July of 2010, Sr. McDuffie retired to Oakwood, the RSCJ retirement home in Atherton, California, where she became an even more avid reader after she acquired a Kindle. She was also the first in her community to use Facebook. When cancer struck her for the second time, in September of 2014, she became determined to go on whale watches – three of them – while she still had the strength to do so. She died on February 20, 2016, and is buried in the Academy cemetery in Grand Coteau.

# Alice Mills, RSCJ
(1931-2017)
*(1975-2014)*

A native Louisianian, Alice Mills was born in Arnaudville, which is just a few miles from Grand Coteau, on October 8, 1931. Losing her mother unexpectedly when Alice was but 14, she understood early in life what it means to lose a loved one. Perhaps this motivated her to pursue a career in counseling and psychology later as an adult.

**Sister Mills**

She attended Arnaudville High School and then became a student at the College of the Sacred Heart in Grand Coteau, where she majored in English. This is where she developed a religious vocation and, after graduation, entered the Society of the Sacred Heart at Kenwood in Albany, New York. She made her first vows in 1955 and final profession in Rome in 1961.

Having a special love for middle-schoolers, she worked in various Sacred Heart prep schools. Believing girls this age need a special time and a place to share, she facilitated small group sessions, providing a safe place for them to talk through their problems and concerns. In the mid-1970s, she moved to Grand Coteau, where she was in service to the Academy and the Thensted Center for 39 years. During this time, in addition to her teaching and general counseling obligations, she became a grief counselor for the Grand Coteau community, a docent for the Saint John Berchmans Shrine, and a trusted confidant of many.

In 2014, after so many years in active service, she retired to Oakwood, the retirement home for the Religious of the Sacred Heart in Atherton, California. There she died on July 20, 2017, surrounded by her religious sisters. She is buried in the Academy cemetery in Grand Coteau.

# Claire Kondolf, RSCJ
(1924-2014)
*(1982-87)*

If Sr. Claire Kondolf, RSCJ, wasn't in her office or somewhere in the school buildings, she was most probably riding a horse around the Academy property. She had a great love for them and she enjoyed riding with the students who boarded their horses or were taking riding lessons.

Born in Bryn Mawr, Pennsylvania, on July 11, 1924, she grew up with an inquisitive mind and a fun-loving spirit. Known as a storyteller and a great conversationalist, she made many long-lasting friendships that endured to the end of her life.

She answered God's call to the religious life and entered the Society of the Sacred Heart in Albany, New York, on September 8, 1947. On March 8, 1950, she professed her first vows and made her final profession in Rome on July 29, 1955.

After working in Sacred Heart schools in New York City, Bryn Mawr, Boston, Bethesda, Miami, and Seattle, she came south to the heart of Cajun Country. It must have been a bit of a culture shock to come to the tiny town of Grand Coteau, Louisiana, after so many years in major cities. However, her years at Coteau as the Headmistress allowed her to further improve the innovative equestrian arts program, to make advances in the curriculum, and to establish the foundation for the Primary School.

**Sister Kondolf**

Her work after Coteau included editing the Society newsletter for 15 years, a ministry at Sprout Creek Farm in Poughkeepsie, New York, and volunteer work in Washington, D.C.

Sr. Claire Kondolf retired at Teresian House in Albany, where she died on January 18, 2014. She is buried at Kenwood.

## Carol Haggarty, RSCJ
### (1941-2017)
*(1992-2001)*

**Sister Haggarty**

Sister Carol Haggarty, a Religious of the Sacred Heart and Academy Headmistress, was known for her loving spirit, her love for God, and her devotion to service within the Sacred Heart Network.

Sr. Haggarty was born on September 14, 1941, in Chicago. She entered the Society in 1961 at the young age of 20, took her first vows in 1964, and made her final profession in Rome in 1969. Along the way she earned a BA in education and an MA in administration and supervision.

Her education allowed her to serve in many positions in numerous Sacred Heart schools, where her loving spirit shone through her multitude of faculty roles, beginning with her time as the middle school assistant principal of the Academy of the Sacred Heart in Chicago in 1969. Later, she served as guidance counselor at Duchesne Academy of the Sacred Heart in Omaha, Nebraska. In 1992, Sr. Haggarty became the Headmistress of the Academy in Grand Coteau and served until 2001. She came in with Hurricane Andrew and left with Tropical Storm Allison!

Sr. Haggarty's dedication and dynamic leadership led to her serving on the provincial team from 1988 to 1993 and again in 2012. Her work earned her numerous leadership opportunities, including as Assistant Executive Director of the Network of Sacred Heart Schools from 2001 to 2012. She also served on several Sacred Heart school boards, including Stuart Country Day School in Princeton, New Jersey; Academy of the Sacred Heart ("The Rosary") in New Orleans; and Villa Duchesne Oak Hill School in St. Louis, Missouri. Over a 20-year period, Sr. Haggarty exhibited her devotion to Sacred Heart education by attending every Network meeting for heads and board chairs. After her return to the Provincial Office in 2012, her ministry within Sacred Heart schools was complete.

Through her untiring service and her strong commitment to furthering the mission of Sacred Heart, Sr. Haggarty's faith and generosity became well-known throughout the Network. After a battle with cancer, she returned to the hands of our loving Father on June 18, 2017, in Atherton, California.

Source: Behrens, Linda. "Carol Haggarty, RSCJ." *Society of the Sacred Heart United States-Canada*, 4 October 2017, https://rscj.org. 12-2-19.

— *Olivia Courville*, Class of 2022

Ms. Burns

# Mary Theodosia Burns
(1942 -2011)
*(2002-07)*

The establishment of Berchmans Academy, a Sacred Heart school for boys, was only one of the more notable accomplishments during the tenure of Ms. Mary Burns, Headmistress. She also welcomed nearly 350 girls to the Academy in the aftermath of Hurricanes Katrina and Rita.

When Hurricane Katrina devastated the Gulf Coast and particularly New Orleans on August 30, 2005, many Sacred Heart students at "The Rosary" in New Orleans found themselves displaced by the accompanying flood waters that stretched over 80 percent of the city. Other students at other schools in the city and along the Gulf Coast were also without a school to attend. Many sought the refuge of the Academy of the Sacred Heart in Grand Coteau.

Ms. Burns opened not only the doors of the Academy to the evacuees, she opened her heart, welcoming them with open arms. With the help of Sr. Lynne Lieux, the Upper School Head from the Rosary, she helped Academy teachers absorb new students into their classrooms and established a satellite school at a nearby facility in Grand Coteau for the Rosary students, who would be taught by some of their regular teachers. (Necessity truly must be the mother of invention: The Rosary faculty set up "classrooms" in the appropriated gym with yellow tape on the floor indicating the sections for the freshmen, sophomores, juniors, and seniors.)

Some students stayed only a few days as their families moved to other towns and cities; others remained a few weeks; The Rosary girls stayed until the beginning of November; and some girls stayed the whole school year. Ms. Burns had informed families to pay what they could when they could. It was a remarkable time in the already-remarkable history of the Academy of the Sacred Heart.

From that commitment to these displaced students came the gift of the portable buildings that became the genesis of Berchmans Academy on the grounds of the Academy. The school was named for St. John Berchmans, who was instrumental in the 1866 miraculous healing of Mary Wilson, a postulant at Grand Coteau. Under Ms. Burns' leadership, the boys' and girls' schools eventually became the Schools of the Sacred Heart.

Ms. Burns left the Academy in 2007 and retired to Gainesville, Florida, where she died after a battle with cancer, on December 14, 2011 – fittingly on the anniversary of the Miracle of Grand Coteau.

**Sister Demoustier**

# Claude Demoustier, RSCJ
(1940-2012)
*(2007-08)*

Marie-Thérèse Claude Demoustier was born on July 31, 1940, in Pointe à Pierre, Trinidad, West Indies, the eldest of five daughters. The child of a Schlumberger engineer, she lived in France, Trinidad, Martinique, the United States, Venezuela, and Switzerland and gained an international outlook on the world, a perspective that served her well.

She was proficient in several languages and had special skills in drawing, design, calligraphy, and sewing. She also possessed a love of reading and sports.

Sr. Demoustier entered the Society of the Sacred Heart on October 20, 1963, at Kenwood in Albany, New York. She professed first vows in April of 1966 and final vows in Joigny, France, September 10, 1972. She became an American citizen in July of 1983. Sister Demoustier taught French, Spanish, English, and religion at several different Sacred Heart schools, including the ones in St. Louis, New Orleans, and Houston. She was Headmistress at Woodlands Academy in Lake Forest, Illinois, from 1991 to 2000, and she later served the International Society of the Sacred Heart's General Council as Secretary General in Rome.

She did, however, have a special connection to the Academy of the Sacred Heart in Grand Coteau. Sr. Demoustier was a student at the Academy in Grand Coteau, where she was introduced to the Society of the Sacred Heart and where she later served as Director of Students and as Headmistress. As Headmistress from 2007 to 2008, Sr. Demoustier is remembered as a strong supporter of Berchmans Academy because of her dedication to the growth and future of the boys' school.

She retired to Oakwood, the Society of the Sacred Heart's elder care facility in Atherton, California, where she passed away on September 2, 2012, of inoperable cancer at the age of 72. She is buried at the Sacred Heart cemetery in Grand Coteau.

Sources:
– https://rscj.org/about/memoriam/claude-demoustier-rscj 11-4-19
– https://patch.com/missouri/ladue-frontenac/claude-demoustier-rscj-of-villa-duchesne-dies-at-age-72 11-4-19

— *Caroline Quebedeau*, Class of 2022

# Glossary

**Acadiana** – The 22 parishes of Louisiana that comprise the region settled by the French-Acadian, or Cajun, people following their exile in 1755 from what is known today as Nova Scotia. Acadiana is located in the southern region of the state and stretches as far west as Calcasieu and Cameron parishes and as far east as Lafourche, St. Charles, and St. John parishes, with Avoyelles Parish being the northernmost. St. Landry Parish, where the Academy of the Sacred Heart is located, is in the heart of Acadiana.

**Aspirant** – A Religious of the Sacred Heart who has made first vows but not yet final profession. This stage of formation is now known as Professed of Temporary Vows. (For a fuller explanation of the stages required to become a Religious, see Appendix 5.)

**Attestation** – Witnessing of an event.

***Buanderie*** – Laundry room or utility room.

**Choir religious** – Old European term for the religious known as **Mother** or **Madame**, who are generally well-educated. They were the teachers and administrators. The term, which was eliminated throughout the Society in 1964, means that these Religious sang or recited the Office "in choir," or as a group.

**Coadjutrix religious** – Old European term for the "working class" religious known as Sister. They did not teach, but did the domestic work of the community. This made religious life possible for many who would not have otherwise been able to attain it. Today, Sister is used for all members of the Society of the Sacred Heart.

***Congé*** – School play days, particularly the Senior *congés*, which are unannounced to surprise the students and engage them in cross-grade activities and *goûter*. Also, a family play day held on the school grounds, often used in later years as a fundraiser.

**Final Profession** – The last step in the process of becoming a religious. (See Appendix 5)

**First vows** – A candidate for the religious life as a member of the Society of the Sacred Heart takes her first vows after being a novice for two years. (See Appendix 5)

***Goûter*** – As a verb, to taste; as a noun, a light meal, usually a sweet treat for students and faculty/staff. Often occurs after a celebratory liturgy or mid- to late afternoon.

***Maîtresse générale du pensionnat*** – Director of the boarding school.

**140** *Glossary*

**Medallion** – A merit award given only in senior year to outstanding student leaders.

**Mistress General** – The term formerly used to identify the **Headmistress**, also known as *Directrice* **or Principal**. The different terms conformed to what various independent schools used at the time.

**Mother General** – The "president" or CEO of the Society, usually called **Superior General** today. She governs with a council of advisors, previously called **Assistants General**, but now **General Council** or **Central Team**. She serves an eight-year term and is headquartered in Rome.

**Mother Provincial** – Commonly referred to as the **Provincial**, she is the leader of a Province and is assisted by her Provincial Team. Grand Coteau is part of the United States-Canada Province, headquartered in St. Louis. (See also Vicar and Vicariate.)

**Mother Superior** – The term was formerly used to identify the leader of an individual RSCJ house, also known as **Superior** or **Reverend Mother**. Since the 1970s the term is no longer used in America.

**Novice** – A person in the second step of the process of becoming a religious. (See Appendix 5)

**Novitiate** – The period of two years in religious life before taking vows; a place housing religious novices.

***Pensionnat*** – French for boarding school. The boarders were known as *pensionnaires*.

**Postulant** –   Now called candidate, a person in the first step of the process of becoming a religious. (See Appendix 5)

***Prise d'habit*** – French term for taking the habit and becoming a novice.

**Prize of Excellence** – An award that was given only when a student met the required high criteria.

**Provincial** – The person in charge of all convents and ministries in a Province.

***Rentrée*** – The return to school at the beginning of an academic year.

**Retreat** – A period of seclusion devoted to prayer and religious contemplation.

**Ribbons** – Awards of merit given to students who meet particular criteria.

**"The Rosary"** – A nickname for the Academy of the Sacred Heart in New Orleans. Like the Academy in Grand Coteau, it is a single-gender girls Catholic school.

**RSCJ** – "*La Société des Religieuses du Sacré Cœur de Jésus*" – These are the initials for the French title Religious of the Sacred Heart of Jesus, which originated in France in 1800.

**Superior General** – Term used today to identify the international head of the Society of the Sacred Heart. (See also Mother General)

**Venerated Mother** – A title of respect, usually referring to a Superior.

**Vicar** – The governor of a regional area in the Society; the term was replaced with the title **Provincial** in 1970.

**Vicariate** – On the regional level, the area governed by a superior vicar with the assistance of consultors. In the 1970s the term was replaced by **Province**.

***Visitatrice*** (alternate *Visitratrix*) – An RSCJ from outside the Province who was appointed by the Superior General to make official visits and report back to the central authority. Now the Superior General or members of her team make the visits.

# Timeline

### *Significant dates in the history*
### *of the Academy of the Sacred Heart at Grand Coteau*

**1821** – Foundation of the Academy of the Sacred Heart is begun at Grand Coteau

**1822** – Month-long visit from Mother Philippine Duchesne

**1823** – Academy's first purchase of an enslaved person, Frank Hawkins

**1829** – Christmas visit from Mother Philippine Duchesne

**1830** – First brick of new building laid

**1831** – Key to new building given to Mother Xavier Murphy (Oct. 15)

**1832** – Cholera rages throughout the district

**1833** – Bishop's Cottage completed

**1834** – Brick building begun for kitchen, *dépense*, vestry, laundry, and housing for three enslaved families

**1835** – 130-foot addition to the main building includes a gallery

**1838** – Jesuits establish a college in Grand Coteau

**1847** – Yellow fever ravages New Orleans

**1848** – RSCJ novitiate opens with four novices and three postulants

**1850** – 100th pupil arrives; enrollment goes to 116, the highest level yet

**1851** – Christmas Mass celebrated in the not-quite-finished Chapel

**1854** – 48 cases of measles in the Boarding School

**1861** – Civil War begins

**1864** – Aid and protection provided by Union General Nathaniel Banks

**1865** – Hostilities cease; Abraham Lincoln is assassinated

**1866** – Miraculous cure of Mary Wilson through the intercession of Blessed John Berchmans (Dec. 14)

**1873** – A room in the former novitiate is converted to the Shrine of St. John Berchmans

**1875** – School for Black girls opened

**1878** – Another yellow fever epidemic ravages the area

**1879** – Boiler room explosion results in death of a novice

**1884** – Students receive permission for the first time ever to spend Christmas holidays at home

**1888** – John Berchmans canonized (Jan. 15)

**1893** – Foundation of new refectory is blessed

**1895** – Rare snow falls for two days (Feb. 14 & 15)

**1896** – Novitiate is closed

**1900** – RSCJ Centenary celebrated, marked by a letter from Pope Leo XIII and festivities till midnight

**1908** – Madeleine Sophie Barat beatified

**1914** – Fire consumes much property; plans are made for a 2-year Normal School; World War I begins

**1918** – Intense cold and snow burst pipes throughout the property; Spanish Flu pandemic takes many lives; Normal School commencement and first diplomas awarded; World War I ends

*Timeline* **143**

**1920** – Fire causes two deaths and one injury of nun on whom a wall collapses

**1921** – Centennial of Academy celebrated

**1924** – Grand Coteau Religious vote in a civic election for the first time

**1925** – Madeleine Sophie Barat canonized (May 25)

**1927** – Great Flood brings hundreds of refugees to the area and to the Academy

**1930** – Central heating is installed

**1937** – New road between the Academy and St. Charles Borromeo Church in Grand Coteau is completed

**1938** – Plans for a Sacred Heart College approved

**1939** – Normal School transitions to a 4-year College, opened with 55 boarders (Sept. 12); World War II begins (Sept. 1)

**1940** – Philippine Duchesne beatified

**1941** – Statue of *Mater* procured for the College and housed in Memorare Hall

**1945** – World War II ends

**1946** – Chapel renovated and new statues of Mary and Joseph installed

**1947** – Hand-carved Stations of the Cross and large Crucifix are installed in the Chapel

**1950** – New gymnasium dedicated (January 8)

**1951** – Ice storm and snow leave school without electricity, heat, and water (except water from the cistern) for 3 days; Lourdes grotto completed and blessed

**1953** – Desegregation begins in Grand Coteau as two Black students are accepted into the College

**1956** – Last graduation from the College (May 31)

**1957** – Hurricane Audrey causes power outage for 30 hours

**1959** – White plaster removed from façade of main building, revealing soft-red brick

**1967** – The Religious change their habits in accordance with guidelines issued by Vatican II

**1968** – 30 students attend celebration in St. Charles, Missouri, for the 150th anniversary of Mother Duchesne's coming to the USA

**1969** – 300 members of the Alumnae Association come to lunch at the Academy and are served by 3rd Academic students costumed in Acadian dress; groundbreaking for new cafeteria

**1970** – Latiolais Hall, the new cafeteria, completed

**1971** – 150 years of continuous education at ASH commemorated

**1982** – Restoration of the front gardens begins

**1987** – Primary School opens, eventually serving classes Pre-K thru 4

**2005** – Hurricanes Katrina and Rita challenge ASH with the influx of nearly 350 displaced students for varying lengths of time

**2006** – Berchmans Academy opens and begins offering classes to boys

**2007** – Tablet PC program implemented to allow off-campus learning during lengthy school closures

**2008** – Hurricane Gustav causes great damage to Academy grounds and nearly every building

**2018** – First formal gathering of descendants of enslaved persons at ASH: "We Speak Your Name"

**2020** – COVID-19 causes an abrupt end to in-class learning for a considerable length of time

**2021** – The Academy of the Sacred Heart celebrates its Bicentennial

## Appendix 1

# The Great Flood of 1927

*Excerpts from the writings describing the Flood of 1927,
found in the* **House Journal, 1926-1941,** *as translated
by Dr. Anna (Laurie) Servaes on Oct. 19, 2019*

## General Situation of the Country
## and Lower Louisiana

Since the month of last September, torrential rains (like we've never seen in the memory of man) fell in 30 of the 48 states that form North America, from the region of the Great Lakes to the Gulf of Mexico. Moreover, the snow was abundant in the Northern states and in Canada, such that the Great Lakes, having been flooded, the rivers to which they give rise were overwhelmed....

The annual and regular rise of the *Père des Eaux* ("The Father of Waters," the Mississippi River) takes place generally in April-May, and usually is retained by the levees.... But these kinds of dykes could not resist the fury of the surge when it is a hundred times over; thus, terrible cracks are produced in the levees which open passage to floods, taking homes, uprooting ancient oaks and rush in their course toward the big spillway of the Gulf of Mexico.

Such is the aspect that is currently presented in the land situated on the two banks of the Mississippi. More than 300,000 people had to leave their homes. Some took refuge at friends' homes or with parents in other states, the majority in camps organized by the Government, where the Committees of the Red Cross provide for the needs of the victims. Secretary of State Hoover put into service of these unfortunates all the resources of his engineering organizer. The camps are divided into small apartments with electricity, kitchen, and sanitary systems of first order.

Thousands of soldiers, convicts, engineers, workers, and landowners work day and night and side by side to strengthen the weak points of the levees or to free the unlucky who found themselves surrounded by the furious elements. The inhabitants of the localities in danger were foreseen, and many were able to leave in time, bringing livestock and furniture. But a great number did not want to abandon their homes, believing they would be able to hold up through the ordeal, and found themselves isolated. Hundreds of rescues are happening each day; trucks, wagons, boats are requisitioned; all the resources and the willing are at the disposition of the Committees. So there is a comparatively small amount of deaths to grieve....

The losses of buildings and animals is incalculable. A fundraising effort of $10 million was proposed and surpassed by much more for help to the flood victims and for compensation. The Government also took preventative measures. In the face of imminent danger that was heading for the city of New Orleans, situated on the estuary of the Mississippi on the Gulf of Mexico, the Government blew up dynamite in a part of the dykes that was found along the passage of the receding waters, in order to make them take another course. The City is thus out of danger, but the swells of water... continue to submerge by the hundreds the small localities that they encounter.

Thanks to this artificial crack, our St. Michael House finds itself a little bit assured of security, the river having earlier lowered in this direction.

But each day or each night the surges break the dykes at unattended places. That is how on May 18 the inhabitants of Melville (situated on the Atchafalaya, a tributary of the Mississippi, small town of about 1,000 inhabitants) were awoken by the bugle and the dire cry, "Crack! Crack!" The water in effect invaded everything, and each one had to escape in bedclothes to reach the boats or wagons that were waiting for the unfortunate. They report that the sick died *en route*, while little Moseses (newborns) were making their entrance into this world.

It is impossible to describe the misery and the consternation of these poor victims; some seem to lose their mind, others persevere to return and to find only ruins. Entire families wait in attics or on roofs or on trees for the arrival of the rescue boats.

Thousands of livestock and poultry... are abandoned and drowned; dogs, cats perched on their former home seem to beg to also be collected; a beautiful deer joined a family that made the boat and was saved. On the trees, instead of birds, you can see snakes in droves....

The waters of this Melville crack spread all over so quickly that they flooded at least 27 small localities in a few days, some very near us, and put hundreds of families in distress.

Our Grand Coteau House is situated on a plateau (its name comes from it), thus it does not have to fear the flooding. But it is surrounded by small towns and localities in which the terrain is very low, and [whose residents] have to flee before the flood. Lafayette and Opelousas are also on elevated ground. They were thus able to establish refugee camps there. The little city of Lafayette that ordinarily has hardly 10,000 inhabitants received more than 21,000 refugees; and Opelousas (5,000 inhabitants) received about 16,000. The individual families, even the poor cabins of the Negros, open up to the flood victims, and they share with joy the meager meal or the abundance of each home.

**The Convent of Grand Coteau** received and housed several families, while livestock by the hundreds graze in our beautiful prairies and in those of St. Charles College. The men and the vehicles of the College and the Convent are at the disposition of the public charity, and fervent prayers are increased each day after the Holy Mass and at the Blessing of the Holy Eucharist to obtain from Heaven the cessation of the terrible curse.

The probable forecast is that the floods will not stop until after mid-June. A number of parents have taken their children home beginning from the middle of May, in fear of not being able to reach the Convent. The father of one of our children coming here in passing brought a rescue barge to help a family taking refuge on the roof of their house (in Prairie Laurent, about three miles away) and who would invariably perish without this help.

In the Diocese of Lafayette alone more than 10 churches or mission chapels are ruined [as are] many schools. What is certainly to fear now are the epidemics that could cause unhealthiness in the water and unhealthy emissions from so much debris and animal cadavers. But the medical corps is watching for the danger and energetic remedies are used without always being successful....

The resignation, the endurance, the dedication, and the charity of the flood victims and the rescuers were, on all points, admirable, and we were able to observe numerous returns to God. In the boarding school of Grand Coteau, as in many other institutions, the rewards and small scholastic triumphs were transformed into help to the victims, to whom were distributed generous alms, in supplies and clothing, as well as tools and seed to begin life again.

Our poor people of the Colored School generously made the sacrifice of their prizes and of their annual fair, but our women anxiously called for their retreat. "We really need to pray," they said. They will be satisfied in the same ways as the Ladies of the World [the adult Children of Mary], for whom we had feared also the impossibility of the Holy Exercises this year.

But the number of members is more considerable than ever, and the Heart of Jesus will see His reign advanced in this country, ... in these days of calamity inasmuch as and maybe more than it was the previous year by the splendid demonstrations of faith of the XXVIII Eucharistic Congress.

[May] the Heart of Jesus and Our Lady of Prompt Succor, Patron Saint of Louisiana, have pity on us, and provide the salvation to so many unfortunates who maybe have forgotten their duties and their dependence on the Creator!

Appendix 2

# Hymns, Prayers and Poems of the Schools of the Sacred Heart

Over the many years of the Academy of the Sacred Heart there has been a long tradition of songs and prayers special to the school community. Many alumnae who have gotten married have often chosen one or more of them for their wedding ceremony, particularly *Coeur de Jesus*. Following are some of the ones prayed and sung for many decades.

### Coeur de Jesus

*Cœur de Jésus sauvez le monde,*
*Que l'univers Vous soit soumis.*
*En Vous seul notre espoir se fonde,*
*Seigneur, Seigneur, Vous nous l'avez promis.*

*Vous l'avez dit, Votre promesse.*
*Fait notre espoir, Notre Bonheur.*
*Je bénirai dans ma tendresse,*
*Les enfants de Mon Sacré Cœur.*

### School Song

We pledge our love to Grand Coteau,
Mid oak and towering pine
O dearest Alma Mater
A glorious task is thine:
To make the future noble,
To make the future noble,
To make the future noble,
That task is thine.

We promise to be faithful to all
That Coteau's taught
To spread the fire of charity
That burns in Coteau's heart
With aims and with ideals,
With aims and with ideals,
With aims and with ideals,
True to the Sacred Heart.

### Saint Madeleine Sophie

See she stands, Saint Madeleine Sophie
Glorious in God's holy place;
Her great soul reflects His splendor,
And the beauty of His face.
Praise be God who wrought from nothing,
All the shining worlds above;
He hath raised a lowly creature,
To the summits of His love.

Look on us, Saint Madeleine Sophie,
Listen to the hymn we raise;
'Tis the praise of God's own glory,
That we sing who sing Thy praise.

Praise be God who wrought from nothing,
All the shining worlds above;
He hath raised a lowly creature,
To the summits of His love.

– Louise Keyes, RSCJ, and C.A. Carroll, RSCJ

## Prayer to St. John Berchmans

John, our brother,
You already enjoy the face-to-face
 vision of God.
Please remember us to Him
as we struggle here on earth
to attain the joy you now possess.
Your life on earth was so much like
 ours
in its simplicity and daily round of
 tasks.
Help us to face these heroically and
 constantly as you did,
so that we become daily more
 pleasing to our Heavenly Father.

**St. John Berchmans**

## Hymn to Saint Philippine

Strong was her heart that heard
 God's voice
When far it called across the sea,
And swiftly came the answer of her
 love
That gave its all triumphantly.
 For thou wert ready, Philippine
To let God's zeal take fire in thee.

Hard was the road beneath her feet,
And long it stretched through
 shadowed years,
 But stronger was the love that led
 her on.
And brave the faith that conquered
 fears.
For God was with thee, Philippine.
 And drew his harvest from thy
 tears.

– M. Williams, RSCJ, and Mary B. Saunders

## St. Madeleine Sophie's Daily Prayer

Give me a heart that is one with your
 own;
A humble heart that knows and loves
 its nothingness;
A gentle heart that holds and calms
 its own anxiety;
A loving heart that has compassion
 for the suffering of others;
A pure heart that recoils even at the
 appearance of evil;
A detached heart that longs for
 nothing other than the goodness of
 heaven;
A heart detached from self-love and
 embraced by the love of God.
Its attention focused on God, its
 goodness its only treasure in time
 and in eternity.

## Act of Consecration to *Mater*

O Mother of Jesus, *Mater Admirabilis*, we come to you asking that you quench our thirst, warm our hearts, dispel our shadows.
We come to you as children in need of a mother's attentive love and care.
O Admirable Mother, the road of life is often hard, and it is not easy to walk steadily along the path marked out for us.
Nor is it easy to love our neighbor as Jesus would have us love.
*Mater*, may your tender love and care for us give us the courage and generosity to love others as you love us.
With confidence, we entrust to your intercession the gift of our lives, and consecrate all that we are to the embrace of your loving heart.
O most Admirable Mother, you who received Gabriel's joyful greeting, pray for us. Amen.

## Philippine Reflections

*Philippine Duchesne's arrival in America*

– *Illustration by Robin (Catherine Blood, RSCJ)*

*Philippine, remind us of the green and growing moments.*
*Take us with you beyond the pain and winter cold*
  *to see you always young at heart.*
*Let us stand with you on the frontiers of our fears,*
  *sure, as you were,*
*that NOW is the acceptable time.*

*Touch us with your gallant spirit*
*that kept its youth until the very end*
*when you ran lightly as a girl to the God of your joy.*

*Your smile fills the words you left us as our heritage:*
*"I give you my heart, my soul and my life – oh, yes, my life –*
  *gladly."*

*Make us daughters of such a mother, Heart of Jesus.*
*Keep us supple in spirit, growing in hope, rooted in your heart.*

*At the scent of water, may the oak break into bud*
*and put forth new branches as when it was first planted*
  *in America*
*In the strong, young heart of Philippine.*

– *Carmen Smith, RSCJ*

Sr. Anna Mae Marheineke, RSCJ, (1917-2013) was one of five Marheineke girls to attend the Academy of the Sacred Heart in St. Charles, Missouri. A nun who was also a poet, she wrote poems about Grand Coteau during her time here as a teacher, and three of them are presented here. Her poems are collected in the book titled *Smile the Sun Around My Heart: The Collected Poems of Anna Mae Marheineke, RSCJ.*

**'And a path and a way shall be there,
and it shall be called the holy way.'**

(Isaiah, 35:8)

*(For the children of Grand Coteau)*

SING
down the avenue
of pines and enter
the Lord's house singing.
Here
are our hands lifted up
in love and liturgy.
Here we bring
our lives in golden cup
and plate;
see our offering
made consecrate.

We kiss in peace,
and an Alleluia path
opens through our hearts,
hallows them
in joy and Christliness.

We go to share
the Eucharist, to walk now
this holy way, to prepare
a pathway in others' lives
for the Lord.

## 'Were It Not That I Have... Dreams'
### (Hamlet)

*(Dedicated to the Coteau children)*

Not bad dreams. Not
the ghoulish kind that stalk
one through the night
and corner one, and walk

wildly into dawn. These dreams
are gentle. Of children who
go shyly up the stairs
and, when I call to them through

many distances away, nod
charmingly and smile the sun
around my heart. Oh, children
can seal my soul in joy, can run

across my life like petals blown
beautiful and free of flower and stem.
Then are my nights merry when
dreams bring them

dancing down the halls, or find
their dark and golden heads bent
to books in classrooms where
I loved them so, where I meant

to fill with infinity of beauty
those eager minds intensely
looking out through wide, grave
  eyes.
So they come, immensely

Comforting, curtsying across
the long, the happy years. I see
them thus in dreams, always gay,
always, I like to think, with love for
  me.

## Southern Sunset
### (at Grand Coteau)

Just above me a new April moon
held cupped in its crescent a star,
    while the sun's last ray
    made a rosy delay
sending opal and mother-of-pearl to
  play
on the slim white moon's curved bar.

I whistled goodnight to a cardinal
  who called
an answer from a dark-branched
  pine.
    All twilight was fraught
    with the beauty I'd caught
from a moon-cupped star and a tall
  pine taut
against a sky like Burgundy wine.

# Appendix 3

# Treasured Recipes
# from the Coteau Family

The preparation and enjoyment of excellent food is very much a part of the spirit of Louisiana, and at the Academy of the Sacred Heart the consumption of "really good food" is an integral part of the school's culture.

This chapter is lovingly dedicated to the late Sister Barbara Moreau, who was well-known for her cooking prowess and was a much-loved member of the Coteau Community. She died in 2019, leaving behind a legacy of love, generosity, unstinting service, and "really good food." Notably, her favorite recipe book was *Coteau Cooks*.

Some of Sr. Moreau's recipes are in this chapter, and so are a few famed candy recipes from Sr. Rose Guidroz as well as acclaimed recipes from the school's cafeteria.

The following are from Sr. Moreau's collection; they were provided by her sister, Paula Chachere.

## Herbed Cheese Spread

- ♦ 1 stick of butter
- ♦ 2 (8-ounce) packs of cream cheese
- ♦ 1 teaspoon of oregano
- ♦ 1/2 teaspoon each of dill, basil, thyme, and cracked pepper
- ♦ 2 cloves of garlic, chopped

1. Cream butter and cream cheese together.
2. Mix-in herbs.
3. Form into ball or put in crock.
4. Refrigerate at least four hours.

Serve with crackers or French bread slices.

## Barbara's Pasta Salad

- ♦ 3 pounds of bowtie pasta
- ♦ 2 tablespoons of salt
- ♦ 2 tablespoons of olive oil
- ♦ 2 bunches of parsley leaves, finely chopped
- ♦ 8 ounces of fresh Parmesan, grated
- ♦ Red wine vinegar or balsamic vinegar and fresh lemon juice to equal ½ cup of liquid
- ♦ Lemon zest
- ♦ 2 cups of toasted pecans, coarsely chopped
- ♦ Salt and pepper, to taste

1. Boil pasta with salt and olive oil till *al dente*; drain and cool.
2. Mix remaining ingredients in with the pasta.

Refrigerate leftovers.

## BAM Fruit Salad

- 1 jar of citrus salad
- 1 can of pineapple
- 1 orange
- Orange zest
- Cherries, grapes, and chopped apples

Combine all ingredients.

Refrigerate leftovers.

## Sweet Potatoes Bayou Portage

- 3/4 pounds of toasted pecans
- 2 24-ounce cans of sweet potatoes (drain one can)
- 16 ounces of fig preserves
- 1 stick of butter, divided
- 4 tablespoons of cane syrup
- 2 teaspoons of Cajun/Creole seasoning

1. Toast pecans in hot pan (large enough to hold all ingredients) for five minutes.
2. Add remaining ingredients.
3. Let cook on medium heat for 35 to 40 minutes.

– Recipe from *The Acadian*, February 2008

## Chicken with 40 Cloves of Garlic

- 1 medium-sized chicken, cut into serving pieces
- 2 tablespoons of olive oil
- 3 or 4 heads of garlic, divided into 40 cloves and peeled
- 1 1/2 cups of chicken broth
- 1/2 cup of dry Chardonnay
- 1 teaspoon of Herbes de Provence
- Salt and pepper, to taste

1. Place chicken pieces in pan and sauté in oil over medium heat until golden.
2. Add garlic and sauté for two minutes.
3. Add liquids, herbs and seasonings.
4. Simmer until chicken is cooked and sauce is reduced, about 30 minutes.

Serve with boiled new potatoes.

Note: Sister Moreau adjusted this recipe when she made the dish and offers the following suggestions: cook longer; add one chopped bell pepper; use some Tony's; mash the garlic; and increase the wine.

– From *The Daily World* 1-19-05

*Two long-time cooks, Loretta Domingue and Bernice Tate, prepare some "really good food" for student and faculty lunch.*

*Sr. Moreau*

## Sr. Moreau's Rum Cake

- 1 box of yellow cake mix with pudding
- 1 (3-ounce) box of instant vanilla pudding mix
- 3/4 cup of water
- 4 eggs
- 1/4 cup of rum or other liqueur (Amaretto, brandy, etc.)
- 1/2 cup of oil

1. Mix all ingredients together.
2. Grease and flour a Bundt pan.
3. Bake mixture for 30 minutes at 350 degrees.

### GLAZE

- 1 stick of butter (or margarine)
- 1 cup of sugar
- 1/4 cup of water
- 1/2 cup of rum

1. Boil butter and sugar together slowly for five to six minutes.
2. Add water and rum.
3. Pour 3/4 of the glaze over hot cake.
4. Turn cake onto serving plate and top with the rest of the glaze.

## Drunken Pork Chops

- 1/4 cup of finely chopped parsley
- 1 clove of garlic, minced
- 1 tablespoon of olive oil
- Salt and pepper, to taste
- 1 teaspoon of fennel seeds
- 4 pork chops
- 1 cup of dry red wine

1. Mix parsley, garlic, olive oil, salt and pepper, and fennel seeds.
2. Place in frying pan with chops on top.
3. Sauté chops for about five minutes per side.
4. Add wine to pan.
5. Cook over low heat for 20 minutes or until wine is evaporated and chops are cooked.

Note: Sr. Moreau suggests seasoning the pork chops first, then proceed with the recipe. She also suggests using only one-half cup of wine.

– *The Times Picayune*, November 13, 1980

## Aunt Barbara's Kahlua

- 4 cups of water
- 1/2 cup of instant coffee
- 3 3/4 cups of sugar
- 4 teaspoons of vanilla
- A fifth of vodka

1. Bring water to boil, mix one-half cup of boiled water with instant coffee and set aside.
2. Add sugar to remaining water and boil slowly for eight minutes.
3. Add coffee mix, vanilla and vodka.

Makes 2 fifths of kahlua.

# Recipes 155

*Sr. Rose Guidroz's candy-making skills extended far beyond her fudge. Her pralines and other treats were sell-outs every week at her candy sales.*

## Sr. Guidroz's Pralines

- 2 cups of white sugar
- 2 cups of brown sugar
- 1 1/3 cups of evaporated milk
- 3/4 stick of butter
- 1/2 teaspoon of salt
- 1 teaspoon of Karo syrup
- 2 heaping teaspoons of marshmallow crème
- 2 to 3 cups of pecan pieces

1. Combine sugars, evaporated milk, butter, salt, and Karo syrup.
2. Cook to soft-ball stage.
3. Remove from heat; add marshmallow crème.
4. Beat until mixture thickens.
5. Add pecans and stir.
6. Test by dropping a spoonful on waxed paper. If praline holds its shape, the pralines are ready.

– *Sr. Rose Guidroz*

## Sr. Guidroz's Chocolate Fudge

- 4 cups of sugar
- 1 teaspoon of salt
- 2 sticks of butter or margarine
- 1 (12-ounce) can of evaporated milk
- 1 (12-ounce) package of chocolate chips
- 1 (7-ounce) container of marshmallow crème
- 2 cups of pecan pieces

1. Combine sugar, salt, butter, and evaporated milk in a saucepan.
2. Bring to soft-ball stage over medium heat.
3. Remove from heat and stir-in chocolate chips until chips are melted.
4. Blend-in marshmallow crème.
5. Add desired amount of pecan pieces and beat mixture until gloss disappears.
6. Pour into a pan lined with buttered foil.
7. Let candy set till it is firm.

– *Sr. Rose Guidroz*

## Grand Coteau's French Bread

- ♦ 1/4 cup of yeast
- ♦ 7 2/3 cups of water, divided
- ♦ 6 tablespoons of sugar
- ♦ 1/8 cup of salt
- ♦ 5 1/2 quarts of flour
- ♦ 1 cup of dry milk, or powdered milk
- ♦ 6 tablespoons of shortening

1. Dissolve yeast in 2 2/3 cups of lukewarm water.
2. Blend dry ingredients in a mixing bowl on low speed.
3. Add shortening.
4. Add 5 cups of water while mixing on low speed with a dough hook for 30 seconds.
5. Add yeast mixture while mixing on low speed for two minutes.
6. Then mix on medium speed for five minutes.
7. Set the bowl of dough in a warm place for about 15 minutes, until it doubles in volume.
8. Divide the dough in 5 pieces, about 1 pound, 12 ounces each. Shape dough into smooth rolls or loaves.
9. Place the loaves crossways on greased baking pan(s) with space between the loaves.
10. Bake at 350 degrees for 25 minutes.

Makes five loaves.

## Sr. Guidroz's Missouri Cheesecake

- ♦ 1 1/2 cups of graham cracker crumbs
- ♦ 1/2 cup of butter, melted
- ♦ 2 cups of sugar, divided
- ♦ Dash of cinnamon
- ♦ 1 pound of cream cheese
- ♦ 3 eggs
- ♦ 1 1/4 teaspoons of vanilla, divided
- ♦ 2 cups of sour cream

1. Combine graham cracker crumbs, butter, 1/4 cup of sugar and cinnamon.
2. Line this mixture into an 8-inch square pan, patting firmly.
3. Bake at 350 degrees for five minutes.
4. Soften cream cheese to room temperature and beat smooth with 1/2 cup of sugar.
5. Add eggs, one at a time, blending well after each addition.
6. Add 1/4 teaspoon of vanilla.
7. Pour this mixture into crust and bake at 350 degrees for 15 to 20 minutes.
8. While cheesecake is cooling, combine sour cream, 1 1/4 cups of sugar, and 1 teaspoon of vanilla.
9. Pour this mixture very gently over the cooled cheesecake.
10. Bake for 10 minutes at 350 degrees.
11. Chill for 24 hours before serving.

*– Sr. Rose Guidroz*

## Grand Coteau's Favorite Chocolate Chip Cookies
### (Bulk recipe)

- ♦ 9 cups of butter or margarine
- ♦ 6 3/4 cups of brown sugar
- ♦ 6 3/4 cups of granulated sugar
- ♦ 18 eggs
- ♦ 4 1/2 teaspoons of salt
- ♦ 9 teaspoons of vanilla
- ♦ 5 quarts plus 1/2 cup of flour
- ♦ 9 teaspoons of baking soda
- ♦ 9 cups of nuts
- ♦ 18 cups of chocolate chips

1. Grease pans lightly
2. Cream butter, brown sugar, granulated sugar, and eggs together.
3. Add the rest of the ingredients and blend well.
4. Spoon by the teaspoonful onto pans, about two inches apart.
5. Bake at 350 degrees for 12 to 15 minutes.

Yields 24 dozen

# Appendix 4

# Administrative Leaders
## Grand Coteau - 1821-2021

This list was painstakingly compiled by Sr. Mary Lou Gavan,
who assists in the Society of the Sacred Heart Archives,
United States-Canada Province.

**1821-25:** Eugénie Audé – Superior, Mistress General

**1825-36:** Anna Xavier Murphy – Superior, Mistress General

**1837-40:** Julie Bazire – Superior, Mistress General

**1841-42:** Maria Cutts – Superior
Monique Lion – Mistress General of the Boarding School
Carmelite Landry – Mistress General of the Orphans

**1842-45:** Maria Cutts – Superior
Monique Lion – Mistress General of the Boarding School

**1846-47:** Maria Cutts – Superior
Monique Lion – Mistress General of the Boarding School
Carmelite Landry – Mistress General of the Day School

**1847-49:** Maria Cutts – Superior
Monique Lion – Mistress General of the Boarding School
Carmelite Landry – Mistress General of the Orphans

**1849-50:** Maria Cutts – Superior
Carmelite Landry – Mistress General of the Orphans

**1850-51:** Maria Cutts – Superior
Carmelite Landry – Mistress General of the Boarding School

Luisa Lévèque - Mistress General of the Orphans

**1851-52:** Maria Cutts – Superior
Carmelite Landry – Mistress General of the Boarding School
Mary Jane Gardiner – Charged with the Orphans

**1853-54:** Maria Cutts – Superior
Luisa Lévèque - Mistress General of the Boarding School

**1855-56:** Anna Shannon – Superior and Mistress General of the Boarding School

**1857-58:** Aloysia Jouve – Superior
Victoria Martinez – Assistant Mistress General

**1858-59:** Aloysia Jouve – Superior
Victoria Martinez – Mistress General

**1860-61:** Aloysia Jouve – Superior
Eugénie Fréret – Mistress General of the Boarding School

**1865-68:** Victoria Martinez - Superior
Eugénie Fréret – Mistress General of the Boarding School

**1868-69:** Victoria Martinez – Superior
Mary Moran – Mistress General of the Boarding School

**1869-71:** Catalog not in the Archives

**1871-74:** Victoria Martinez – Superior
Isaure Louaillier - Mistress General of the Boarding School

**1874-75:** Mary Moran – Superior
Isaure Louaillier - Mistress General of the Boarding School

**1875-77:** Mary Moran – Superior
Sara Burges - Mistress General of the Boarding School

**1877-78:** Mary Moran – Superior
Emma Chaudet - Mistress General of the Boarding School

**1878-79:** Mary Moran – Superior
Armide Guidry - Mistress General of Boarding School

**1879-81:** Emily Gardner – Superior
Armide Guidry - Mistress General of the Boarding School

**1881-83:** Stanislas Tommasini – Superior
Anna Fréret – Mistress General of the Boarding School

**1883-84:** Emma Chaudet – Superior
Anna Fréret – Mistress General of the Boarding School

**1884-86:** Emma Chaudet – Superior
Mathalie Pujos – Mistress General of the Boarding School

**1886-87:** Emma Chaudet – Superior
Felicia Rigues - Mistress General of the Boarding School

**1887-88:** Emma Chaudet – Superior
Elizabeth Faget - Mistress General of the Boarding School

**1888-89:** Micaela Fesser – Superior
Felicia Rigues - Mistress General of the Boarding School

**1889-92:** Micaela Fesser – Superior
Louise Nadau du Treil – Mistress General of the Boarding School

**1892-97:** Emma Chaudet – Superior
Amalia Tauzin – *Sous* Mistress General of the Boarding School

**1897-99:** Coralie Caisso - Superior
Amalia Tauzin – Mistress General of the Boarding School

**1899-1900:** Henriette Sarens – Superior
Margaret Lyons - *Sous* Mistress General of the Boarding School

**1900-01:** Henriette Sarens – Superior
Margaret Lyons - *Sous* Mistress General of the Boarding School
Teresa Gough – Mistress General of the Parish School
Camille Zéringue - Charged with the school for "*enfants de couleur*"

**1901-02:** Emily Deighton – Superior
Margaret Lyons - Mistress General of the Boarding School
Teresa Gough – Mistress General of the Parish School
Camille Zéringue - Charged with the school for "*enfants de couleur*"

**1902-06:** Emily Deighton – Superior
Mary Fitzwilliam - *Sous* Mistress General of the Boarding School
Teresa Gough – Mistress General of the Parish School
Mary Tayon - Charged with the school for "*enfants de couleur*"

**1906-08:** Marie Bernot – Superior
Mary Fitzwilliam - Mistress General of the Boarding School
Teresa Gough – Mistress General of the Parish School
Mary Tayon - Charged with the school for "*enfants de couleur*"

**1908-09:** Marie Bernot – Superior
Élsabeth Faget - Mistress General of the Boarding School
Teresa Gough – Mistress General of the Parish School
Mary Tayon - Charged with the school for "*enfants de couleur*"

**1909-12:** Marie Bernot – Superior
Nora Farley - Mistress General of the Boarding School
Teresa Gough – Mistress General of the Parish School
Mary Tayon - Charged with the school for "*enfants de couleur*"

*Administrative Leaders* **159**

**1912-13:** Mary Fitzwilliam – Superior
Fanny Savorelli – Charged with the school for "*enfants de couleur*"

**1913-14:** Mary Fitzwilliam – Superior
Virginia Dunn – Mistress General of the Parish School
Camille Zeringue – Charged with the school for "*enfants de couleur*"

**1914-16:** Mary Fitzwilliam – Superior
Antoinette Boland – Mistress General of the Boarding School
Catherine O'Connor – Mistress General of the Parish School
Margaret Kelly – Charged with the school for "*enfants de couleur*"

**1916-1917:** Mary Fitzwilliam – Superior
Mary Gilmore – Mistress General of the Boarding School
Catherine O'Connor – Mistress General of the Parish School
Fanny Savorelli – Charged with the school for "*enfants de couleur*"

**1917-18:** Mary Fitzwilliam - Superior
Mary Gilmore - Mistress General of the Boarding School
Catherine O'Connor – Charged with the Parish School
Fanny Savorelli - Charged with the school for "*enfants de couleur*"

**1918-19:** Marguerite Ducreux – Superior
Catherine Warren - *Sous* Mistress General of the Boarding School
Catherine O'Connor – Charged with the Parish School
Fanny Savorelli - Charged with the school for "*enfants de couleur*"

**1919-20:** Marguerite Ducreux – Superior
Virginia Dunn - Mistress General of the Boarding School
Catherine O'Connor – Charged with the Parish School
Fanny Savorelli - Charged with the school for "*enfants de couleur*"

**1921-23:** Marguerite Ducreux – Superior
Virginia Dunn – Mistress General

**1923-24:** Marguerite Ducreux – Superior
Paméla Doizé – Mistress General

**1924-25:** Marguerite Ducreux – Superior
Virginia Dunn – Mistress General of the Boarding School and the College (2-year)

**1925-26:** Mary Bannantine – Superior
Paméla Doizé – Mistress General of the Boarding School and the College (2-year)

**1926-27:** Mary Bannantine – Superior
Mary Fitzwilliam – Mistress General of the Boarding School
Mary Lynch – Charged with the College (2-Year)

**1927-28:** Mary Bannantine – Superior
Mary Fitzwilliam – Mistress General
Mary Lynch – Directress of the College (2-year)

**1928-29:** Mary Bannantine – Superior
Mary Fitzwilliam – Mistress General

**1929-32:** Mary Fitzwilliam - Superior & Mistress General

**1932-34:** Mary Fitzwilliam – Superior
Mary Greiwe – Mistress General

**1934-35:** Frances Sullivan – Superior
Lily Grace – Mistress General

**1935-36:** Mary Fitzwilliam – Superior
Lily Grace – Mistress General

**1936-37:** Mary Fitzwilliam – Superior
Paméla Doizé – Directress of the College (2-year)
Mary Rueve – Mistress General

**1937-42:** Mary Fitzwilliam – Superior
Mary Rueve – Mistress General

**1942-44:** (Second World War)

**1945-46:** Mary Fitzwilliam – Superior
Marjorie Erskine – Directress of the College (4-year)
Alvena Schraubstader – Mistress General

**160** *Appendix*

**1946-47:** Lucille Walsh – Superior
Marjorie Erskine – President of the College (4-year)
Alvena Schraubstader – Mistress General

**1947-48:** Lucille Walsh – Superior
Marjorie Erskine – President of the College (4-year)
Harriet Corrigan – Mistress General

**1948-49:** Lucille Walsh – Superior
Marjorie Erskine – President of the College (4-year)
Alvena Schraubstader – Mistress General

**1949-51:** Lucille Walsh – Superior
Marjorie Erskine – President of the College (4-year)
Harriet Corrigan – Mistress General

**1951-52:** Lucille Walsh – Superior
Marjorie Erskine – President of the College (4-year)
Claire Saizan – Mistress General

**1952-56:** Odile Lapeyre – Superior
Marjorie Erskine – President of the College (4-year)
Claire Saizan – Mistress General

**1956-58:** Odile Lapeyre – Superior
Anita Villeré – Mistress General

**1958-60:** Katharyn Curtin – Superior
Anita Villeré – Mistress General

**1960-64:** Marjorie Erskine – Superior
Carolyn Mouton – Mistress General

**1964-65:** (No Catalog)

**1965-67:** Antonia Plauché – Superior
Anita Villeré – Mistress General

**1967-68:** Antonia Plauché – Superior
Rita Karam – Mistress General

**1968-71:** Anita Villeré – Superior
Rita Karam – Directress of the School

**1971-73:** Zita St. Paul – Superior
Rita Karam – Principal of the School

**1973-75:** Adele Caire – Coordinator of the Community
Mary Pat Rives – Principal of the School

**1975-76:** Adele Caire – Coordinator
Lucie Nordmann – Principal of the School

**1976-77:** (No Catalog)

**1977-79:** Alice Mills – Coordinator of the *Cor Unum* Community (School building)
Antonia Plauché – Coordinator of the *Joigny* Community (Retirement)
Sharon Karam – Coordinator of the Open House Community (Cottage)
Lucie Nordmann – Principal of the School

**1979-82:** Alice Mills – Coordinator of the *Cor Unum* Community (School building)
Antonia Plauché – Coordinator of the *Joigny* Community (Retirement)
Lucie Nordmann – Coordinator of the Open House Community (Cottage), and Principal of the School

**1982-85:** Alice Mills – Area Coordinator
Eleanor Adams – Coordinator of the *Joigny* Community
Claire Kondolf – Principal of the School

**1985-87:** Alice Mills – Area Coordinator
Claire Kondolf – Principal of the School

**1987-88:** Alice Mills – Area Director
Sally Rude – Headmistress of the School

**1988-89:** Sally Rude – Headmistress of the School

**1989-90:** Joan Ewing – Area Director
Sally Rude – Headmistress of the School

**1990-91:** Pending - Area Director
Sally Rude – Headmistress of the School

**1991-92:** Margaret Mary Hoffman – Area Director
Sally Rude – Headmistress of the School

**1992-94:** Alice Mills – Area Director
Carol Haggarty – Headmistress of the School

*Administrative Leaders* **161**

**1994-96:** Melanie Guste, Anne Byrne – Area Directors
Carol Haggarty – Headmistress of the School

**1996-97:** Kathleen Church, Anne Byrne – Area Directors
Carol Haggarty – Head of School

**1998-2002:** Anne Byrne – Area Director
Carol Haggarty – Head of School

**2002-07:** Anne Byrne – Area Director
Ms. Mary Burns – Head of School

**2007-08:** Anne Byrne – Area Director
Claude Demoustier – Head of School

**2008-09:** Margaret Caire – Area Director
Lynne Lieux – Headmistress

**2009-15:** Georgeann Parizek – Area Director
Lynne Lieux – Headmistress

**2015-16:** Sharon Karam & Lynne Lieux – Regional Convenors
Mr. Michael Baber – Headmaster

**2016-21:** Sharon Karam & Lynne Lieux – Regional Convenors
Dr. Yvonne Adler – Head of School

# Appendix 5

# To become a Religious
# of the Sacred Heart...

When a woman desired to become a Religious, she followed a traditional path to religious life until Vatican II modernized the process. Before then, the procedure was prescribed as follows.

First, one entered the novitiate as a **postulant** for a period of about six months, then received the habit and became a **novice** for two years, although there are instances in the early years of the shortening of that time.

After that, she made **first vows** and became an **aspirant**, usually for five years, but, again, sometimes for a shorter period. The next step in formation was called **probation**, which normally took place in the Mother House in Paris, and then in Rome when Rome became the location of the Mother House. At the end of that, she made **final profession**.

Since 1964, one enters as a **candidate** living in community, then becomes a **novice** for two years, followed by **first vows** for about five years. At this stage in formation, she is known as a **Young Professed** or **Professed of Temporary Vows**. At the end of this period of formation, she goes to Rome for **probation** for four months and then makes her **final profession**.

For a time in the 1970s and 1980s, there were exceptions to the Rome location, with some making their probation in the United States or in international locations like the Philippines or Japan. Now all go to Rome except in some extraordinary circumstances.

Another consequence of Vatican II was a change in the habit worn. The 1960s saw several changes in the attire worn by the Religious of the Sacred Heart with the "new" habit debuting in 1967 and lasting a few years. Now the habit is optional. An example of the habit worn for most of the 19th century and into the 20th century is on display in the museum located on the second floor of the main building of the Academy of the Sacred Heart in Grand Coteau.

# Appendix 6

# Giving Opportunities

Gifts to Sacred Heart, both financial donations and volunteer service, allow the Academy to realize its mission and uphold the 5 Goals that are the foundation of all that the school does and teaches. For this, the Academy of the Sacred Heart remains profoundly grateful.

## Annual Giving

This yearly effort begins July 1 and concludes on June 30, with a goal to raise unrestricted funds for Sacred Heart's operating budget. These funds specifically help to bridge the gap between tuition and the actual cost of a student's education and provide monies that are used immediately for the critical needs of the school.

A gift makes an immediate impact on students and teachers and ensures a distinctive, single-gender, Catholic learning experience that fosters faith, intellect, service, community, and character for a lifetime.

Each year, for the vitality of the school, all members of the Sacred Heart community – from alumnae to parents to Board members to faculty and staff – are asked to prayerfully consider their ability and make their donation to continue the legacy of excellence for the next generation of Sacred Heart scholars.

## Scholarships

The gift of a Sacred Heart education is the gift of a lifelong love of learning. One can share the legacy of this education through contributions to various scholarship funds. The funds include:

- Carmen deMoya Athletic Award Fund
- Msgr. Paul W. Fusilier Scholarship Fund
- Marie Julia Moreau Memorial Scholarship Fund
- Sr. Mathilde McDuffie Scholarship Fund
- RSCJ Scholarship Fund
- Sr. Claire Saizan Scholarship Fund
- Msgr. Alexander O. Sigur Academic Fund
- Thibodeaux-Roy Scholarship Fund
- Rita and Adrian Vega Scholarship Fund
- Sevil Petitjean Scholarship Fund
- Irene Petitjean Scholarship Fund
- Fr. Coyle Scholarship Fund
- Sr. O. Mouton Scholarship Fund
- Historical Buildings Maintenance Fund
- Cindy Leger Memorial Fund
- Sybil F. Boizelle Fund
- Sr. Lieux Scholarship Fund
- The Sacred Heart Fund
- Sr. Barbara Moreau Scholarship Fund
- Adrien and Charles Stewart Scholarship Fund
- STEM Scholarship

## Coteau Remembers

One can honor or celebrate a major milestone, loved one, or someone in need with a donation to Coteau Remembers. Each donation, regardless of size, will ensure that the dedicated intention is inscribed in Coteau Remembers and kept in the prayers of the entire school community.

Corresponding cards will be sent to the recipients to let them know that they have been inscribed in Coteau Remembers.

### Sacred Heart Gallery Restoration

The Academy and Berchmans Academy have begun a campaign to fund the restoration of the gallery of the main building through the sale of commemorative bricks. Benches and plaques are also part of the new project that will not only help to restore the gallery but will add to the beauty of the existing gardens. The bricks and benches will surround the statue of Jesus that is the focal point of the gardens with the inscribed bricks laid at His feet.

### Planned Gifts

Planned gifts include contributions made through a will, charitable gift annuities, charitable trusts, gifts of life insurance, and gifts of retirement plans.

A planned gift helps Sacred Heart ensure its future, enabling the school to expand existing programs and create new programs. While vital to the school, a gift can also help further one's financial and charitable goals. Bequests both large and small have been vital to Sacred Heart since its founding. Many faithful friends have remembered Sacred Heart in their wills while still providing for their families. A bequest through a will also provides continuing support of the ongoing work of the Academy and Berchmans.

*Persons interested in supporting the Academy should contact the Office of the Director of Advancement or the Office of the Director of Alumnae Relations.*

# Sources

"Academy of the Sacred Heart." Grand Coteau, Louisiana. Transcript in general circulation.

Angers, Trent. *Grand Coteau: The Holy Land of South Louisiana*. Lafayette, Louisiana: Acadian House Publishing, 2005.

— *The Miracle of Grand Coteau*. Lafayette, Louisiana: Acadian House Publishing, 2019.

Angers, Trent, Ed. *A Place Set Apart: The Spiritual Journey of Our Lady of the Oaks Jesuit Retreat House*. Lafayette, Louisiana: Acadian House Publishing, 2018.

*Attestation of Sr. Mary Wilson Concerning her Miraculous Cure through the Intercession of Blessed John Berchmans*. Grand Coteau, Louisiana, February 15, 1867.

Blish, Mary, RSCJ, and Carolyn Osiek, RSCJ. *Anna Xavier Murphy, RSCJ: (1793-1836) Missionary to Louisiana*. Society of the Sacred Heart: St. Louis, Missouri, 2021.

Callan, Louise, RSCJ. *The Society of the Sacred Heart in North America*. London: Longmans, Green and Co., 1937.

— *Philippine Duchesne: Frontier Missionary of the Sacred Heart 1769-1852*. Westminster, Maryland: The Newman Press, 1857.

Chicoine, Maureen, RSCJ, https://rscj.org/the-story-of-the-enslaved-persons-of-the-convent-of-the-sacred-heart-grand-coteau-louisiana-1821.

*Coteau Cooks: A Book of Favorite Recipes*. Leawood, Kansas: Circulation Service, Inc., 1988.

*Coteau Cooks II: A Collection of Recipes by Academy of the Sacred Heart*. Kearney, Nebraska: Morris Press Cookbooks, 2004.

Cunningham, Ruth, RSCJ. *The Untold Story: Eugénie Audé, RSCJ*. Society of the Sacred Heart, United States Province, 1986.

"Disciplinary Regulations," *Memorial Journal 1918-1939*. Series IV. St. Louis Province: Grand Coteau, 3. School, l. College, Box 1, Packet II. Society of the Sacred Heart, Canadian and United States Province Archives, St. Louis, Missouri (SSH Provincial Archives, Canada/USA), St. Louis, Mo.

Everson, Erin. "At the heart of dialogue." *Heart: A Journal of the Society of the Sacred Heart, United States – Canada*. Vol. 16, No. 2, 2019: 10-13.

"Gifts Presented by the Graduates," *Memorial Journal 1918-1939*. Series IV. St. Louis Province: Grand Coteau, 3. School, l. College, Box 1, Packet II. Society of the Sacred Heart, Canadian and United States Province Archives, St. Louis, Missouri (SSH Provincial Archives, Canada/USA), St. Louis, Mo.

Gimber, Frances, RSCJ. *Saintes Savantes: Religious of the Sacred Heart in Higher Education*. http://www.rscj.org/religious-sacred-heart-higher-education, January 14, 2020.

"A History of the Academy of the Sacred Heart, Grand Coteau, Louisiana 1821-1971." Grand Coteau, Louisiana. Transcript in general circulation.

**166** *Sources*

Marheineke, Anna Mae, RSCJ. *Smile the Sun Around My Heart*. St. Charles, Missouri: Academy of the Sacred Heart Alumni Association, 2005.

Martinez, Marie Louise, RSCJ, Ed. *"Southward Ho!" The Society of the Sacred Heart enters "Lands of the Spanish Sea."* St. Louis, Missouri: The Society of the Sacred Heart, United States Province, 2003.

Neyrey, Jerome, SJ, and Thomas Clancy, SJ. *Southern Jesuit Biographies: Pastors and Preachers, Builders and Teachers of the New Orleans Province*. Lafayette, Louisiana: Acadian House Publishing, 2015.

"Recommendations," *Memorial Journal 1918-1939*. Series IV. St. Louis Province: Grand Coteau, 3. School, l. College, Box 1, Packet II. Society of the Sacred Heart, Canadian and United States Province Archives, St. Louis, Missouri (SSH Provincial Archives, Canada/ USA), St. Louis, Mo.

Schmidt, K. L. (2020). A National Legacy of Enslavement: An Overview of the Work of the Slavery, History, Memory, and Reconciliation Project, *Journal of Jesuit Studies*, 8(1), 81-107. doi: https://doi.org/10.1163/22141332-0801P005.

Townsend, Katharine, RSCJ, Translator. *House Journal 1821-1884: English Translation*. Grand Coteau, Louisiana, 1976.

Williams, Margaret. *Second Sowing: The Life of Mary Aloysia Hardey*. New York: Sheed & Ward, 1942.

# References

### Chapter 1. The Birth of a Legacy

1. *House Journal 1821-1884*, 1803
2. *House Journal 1821-1884*, 1819
3. *House Journal 1821-1884*, 1821
4. Callan, Louise, RSCJ, *Society of the Sacred Heart...*, 116
5. Cunningham, Ruth, RSCJ. *The Untold Story...,* 27
6. Cunningham, 117
7. Cunningham, 31
8. *House Journal 1821-1884*, 1821
9. Ibid.

### Chapter 2. From Small Beginnings

1. *House Journal 1821-1884*, 1821
2. *House Journal 1821-1884*, 1822
3. *House Journal 1821-1884*, 6-6-1822
4. Callan, *Society*, 126
5. Callan, *Society*, 126-127
6. Callan, *Society*,147
7. *House Journal 1821-1884*, 1-1-1852
8. Ibid.
9. Callan, *Society*, 132
10. Cunningham, 37
11. Ibid.

### Chapter 3. The Campus Expands

1. *House Journal 1821-1884*, 9-30-1830
2. Callan, *Society*, 140
3. *House Journal 1821-1884*, 1-28-1833

### Chapter 4. The Jesuits Settle in Grand Coteau

1. Callan, *Society*, 152
2. *House Journal 1821-1884*, 6-21-1837
3. Ibid.

4. Ibid.
5. Callan, *Society*, 152
6. Ibid.
7. *House Journal 1821-1884*, 12-25-1838

### Chapter 5. Slavery in Antebellum Times

1. *House Journal 1821-1884*, 1821
2. Chicoine, Maureen, RSCJ, "The Story of the Enslaved Persons…"
3. *House Journal 1821-1884*, 6-26-1829
4. *House Journal 1821-1884*, 8-15-1829
5. *House Journal 1821-1884*, 1-28-1835
6. *House Journal 1821-1884*, 12-8-1829
7. *House Journal 1821-1884*, 12-15-1834
8. Ibid.
9. Chicoine, Maureen, RSCJ
10. Schmidt, K. L. (2020). A National Legacy of Enslavement…
11. *House Journal 1821-1884*, 8-15-1840
12. *House Journal 1821-1884*, 2-9-1842
13. *House Journal 1821-1884*, 1-13-1841
14. *House Journal 1821-1884*, 8-16-1852
15. Chicoine, Maureen, RSCJ

### Chapter 6. Civil War and the Academy

1. *House Journal 1821-1884*, 8-31-1843
2. Callan, *Society*, 519
3. Ibid.
4. Callan, *Society*, 525
5. Callan, *Society*, 526
6. Callan, *Society*, 527
7. Ibid.
8. Callan, *Society*, 528
9. *House Journal 1821-1884*, 170
10. *House Journal 1821-1884*, Dec. 1864
11. Callan, *Society*, 539

**168** *References*

### Chapter 7. The Miracle of Grand Coteau

1. *House Journal 1821-1884*, 12-14-1866
2. *Attestation of Sr. Mary Wilson...*, 6
3. *Attestation of Sr. Mary Wilson...*, 9
4. *Lettres Annuelles*, 399

### Chapter 8. Educating a Newly Freed People

1. *House Journal 1821-1884*, 1862
2. Callan, *Society*, 539
3. Ibid.
4. Callan, *Society*, 540
5. Callan, *Society*, 541
6. *House Journal 1821-1884*, 5-3-1875

### Chapter 10. The 19th Century Comes to an End

1. *House Journal 1821-1884*, 10-21-1865
2. *House Journal 1821-1884*, 1872
3. *House Journal 1821-1884*, 11-30-1882

### Chapter 11. A New Century

1. Callan, *Society*, 708-9
2. Callan, *Society*, 772

### Chapter 12. Growth of 'The House of Grand Coteau'

1. Callan, *Society*, 145

### Chapter 13. Normal School and College of the Sacred Heart

1. Gimber, Frances, RSCJ. *Saintes Savantes: Religious of the Sacred Heart...*, 13
2. "Recommendations," *Memorial Journal 1918-1939*
3. "Disciplinary Regulations," *Memorial Journal 1918-1939*

4. "Gifts Presented by the Graduates," *Memorial Journal 1918-1939*
5. *House Journal 1939*, Box 1, 247-248
6. *Memorare 1956*, 20
7. Rives, *Email of Aug. 16, 2019*
8. Moser, *Email of Aug. 30, 2019*

### Chapter 14. The World War II Years

1. *House Journal 1926-1941*, Box 3, 261
2. *House Journal 1926-1941*, Box 3, 277
3. *House Journal 1926-1941*, Box 3, 279
4. *House Journal 1941-1953*, Box 3, 20
5. *House Journal 1941-1953*, Box 3, 23
6. *House Journal 1941-1953*, Box 3, 65
7. *House Journal 1941-1953*, Box 3, 82
8. *House Journal 1941-1953*, Box 3, 90
9. *House Journal 1941-1953*, Box 3, 98
10. *House Journal 1941-1953*, Box 3, 126
11. *House Journal 1941-1953*, Box 3, 130
12. *House Journal 1941-1953*, Box 3, 132

### Chapter 16. Sacred Heart GOALS and CRITERIA

1. Network, RSCJ.org. Sept. 2, 2019
2. Ibid.

### Chapter 17. Toward a Noble future

1. Sacred Heart GOALS and CRITERIA (See Chapter 16)

### Chapter 18. Traditions, Customs & Activities

1. *House Journal 1821-1884*, 1822
2. *A History of the Academy of the Sacred Heart...*, 5
3. *House Journal 1821-1884*, 10-3-1852

## Chapter 19. The Saints
## of the Sacred Heart

1. Callan, Louise, RSCJ, *Philippine Duchesne: Frontier Missionary…*, 30
2. Callan, *Philippine*, 78
3. Ibid
4. Callan, *Philippine*, 113
5. Callan, *Philippine*, 114
6. https://www.kshs.org/kansapedia/rose-philippine-duchesne/16877
7. *House Journal 1926-1941*, Box 3, 263-264
8. Ibid

## Chapter 20. Women of Faith
## and Influence

1. Cunningham, 76
2. *House Journal 1821-1884*, 1-1-1852
3. *House Journal 1821-1884*, Aug. 1854
4. *House Journal 1821-1884*, 12-19-1852
5. Martinez, 83
6. Martinez, 147
7. Martinez, 152
8. Martinez, 103

# Index

**Note:** Page references in **bold** refer to photographs, illustrations, maps, and captions.

**A**bbadie, Fr. John Francis, 30, **30**
Academy of the Sacred Heart - Grand Coteau
   *See also specific topics*; Colored School of the
    Sacred Heart; Religious of the Sacred Heart
    of Jesus (*La Société du Sacré Coeur de
    Jésus*); Saint Peter Claver School
   administrative leaders, 117-137; 157–161
   and Civil War, *iv*, 35, 36–41, 46, 75, 122, 124, 142
   College, 74, 75–77, **76**
   *congé* (play day, fun day), 17, 35, 66, 80, 102,
    **102**, 103, 121, 139
   and Covid-19 quarantine, 95, **96**, 143
   desegregation of, 76, 143
   early history, 15–18, 20–23
   in early twentieth century, 59–61
   expansion, 24–28, 62–73
   founding of, 10, 13
   gifts, giving, opportunities, 163–164
   Goals and Criteria, *vii*, 51, 83, 87–93, 96, 101, 163
   *goûter* (snack, treat), 103, **103**, 132, 139
   hymns, 147–151
   as Institute for the Education of Young Ladies, 17
   and Jesuits, **25**, 28, 29–30, 31, 36, 121
   in late nineteenth century, 55–56
   leaders, administrative, 117–137; 157–161
   map of, **60**
   and Miracle of Grand Coteau, 42–45, 116, 122,
    125, 136
   Normal School, 74–77, 142–143
   photos of, **16, 18–19, 22, 25–26, 27–28, 32, 45,
    62–73, 76, 83, 95–96, 98–106**
   poems, 99, 127, 150–151
   prayers, 53, 147–151
   Primary School, 83, 102–103, 134, 143
   recipes, 152–156
   and The Rosary (Network of Sacred Heart
    Schools sister school), 55, 74, 76, **86**, 93, **94**,
    129, 130, 135–136
   saints of. *See* Barat, St. Madeleine Sophie,
    RSCJ; Berchmans, St. John; Duchesne,
    Mother Rose Philippine, RSCJ
   scholarships, 163

   slavery and, 17, 20–21, 26, 31–35, **33**, 37, 46,
    50–51, **51**
   timeline, 142–143
   traditions, customs, activities, 99–106
   and Vatican II, **56**, 82, **82**, 83, **83**, 87, 143, 162
   World War II and, 75, 78–82, 143
Adler, Yvonne Sandoz, *iv*, 161
administrative leaders, 117–137; 157–161
African Americans. *See* Blacks; slavery
Aubert, Fr. Jean-Baptiste, 111–112
Audé, Etienne, 14
Audé, Mother Eugénie, RSCJ, *iv*, 13–15, **15**, **16**,
   17, 20, 23, 31, **35**, 64, **84**, 117–119, 157

**B**anks, General Nathaniel, *vi*, 37, 39, **39**, 40, 124, 142
Barat, Jacques, 107
Barat, Louis, 107–108, 114
Barat, Marie-Madeleine, 107
Barat, St. Madeleine Sophie, RSCJ, *iv*, 12–15,
   18, 36, 41, 54, 59, 107–110, **108–109**, 113–114,
   117–118, 120, 142–143
Baron, Elisa, 17
Baron, Laura, 17
Bazire, Mother Julie, RSCJ, 28–29, 121–122
Bellanger, Fr., 47
Berchmans, St. John, 42–45, **43–44, 96, 115,** 115–116,
   122–124, 131, 134, 136, 142, 148, **148**
   and Miracle of Grand Coteau, 42–45, 116, 122,
    125
Berchmans Academy of the Sacred Heart, 51, 93,
   **93**, 94, 102–103, 136–137, 143, 164
"Between the Daylight and the Dark" (Smith, Sr.
   Carmen), 127
Bishop's Cottage, 24, 30, 62, 81, 133, 142
Blacks
   *See also* slavery
   education of
     after emancipation, 46–49
     Colored School of the Sacred Heart, 47–48,
      **49**, 78, 80–81, 122, 146
     at Sacred Heart Parochial School (now St.
      Ignatius Elementary School), 48
     Saint Peter Claver School, 48, **49, 81, 83**

*Index* **171**

in twentieth, twenty-first centuries, 48–51
enslaved people. *See* slavery
and Sisters of the Holy Family, 48, 81, **81**
and St. Charles Borromeo Parish, 48, 50
Blessed John Berchmans. *See* Berchmans, St. John
Blood, Catherine "Robin," RSCJ, 149, 177
Bossuet, Bishop, 27
Bourke, Jane, 77
*bousillage*, 27
Burgess, Mr., 24
Burns, Ms. Mary Theodosia, **98**, 136, **136**, 161
Burrus, Fr. Ernest Joseph, SJ, 78, **78**
Butler, General Benjamin, 37

Cain, Lillian, 128
Caire, Elia, 127
Callan, Louise, RSCJ, 37, 59
Carroll, C.A., RSCJ, 147
Castille, Ana, 120
Cervantes, 107
Chachere, Gladys Richard Wheat, 77
Chachere, Paula Moreau, 131, 152
Chaudet, Mother Emma Marie Louise, RSCJ, 124, 158
Cheeran, Hannah, 126, 178
Children of Mary (sodality), 30, **30**, 41, 52, 56, 75, 146
and Ladies of the World (adult Children of Mary), 36, 146
Chretien, Hypolite, 26
Christmas at Coteau, 64, **69**, 103–104, **104**
Civil War, *iv*, 36–41, 46
*Clarissa* (Richardson), 107
*Code Noir*, 31
Colored School of the Sacred Heart, 47–48, **49**, 78, 80–81, 122, 146
*congé* (play day, fun day), 17, 35, 66, 80, **102,** 102–103, 121, 139
Congregation of the Children of Mary, 108
Connelly, Cornelia, 24
Connelly, Pierce, 24
Convent, La., 20, **38**, 47, 64, 117
Coriolis, Mother Josephine, de, RSCJ, 52, 54
Corley, Caroline, 124, 178
Courville, Olivia, 135, 178
Covid-19 quarantine, 95, **96**, 143
Coyle, Fr. Auguste, SJ, 76, 81, 163
Cutts, Mother Maria, RSCJ, 16, 121, 157

De Mérode, Msgr., 41
De Neckere, Msgr., 24
Déjean, Sr. Josephine, RSCJ, 36
Delille, Mother Henriette, SSF (Sisters of the Holy Family), **81**
Demoustier, Sr. Marie-Thérèse Claude, RSCJ, 137, **137**, 161
desegregation, 76, 143
Diaz, Carmen, 77
Domingue, Loretta, **153**
*Don Quixote* (Cervantes), 107
Dorival, Mother Louise, RSCJ, 20, 24, **27**, 120
DuBourg, Bishop William, 114, 119–120
DuBourg, Msgr. William Louis, 13, 20
Duchesne, Charlotte-Euphrosine, 123
Duchesne, Marie-Madeleine, 112
Duchesne, Mother Rose Philippine, RSCJ (St. Philippine Duchesne), *iv*, 13–14, **15, 22**, 22–23, 36, 79, 108, **111**, 111–115, 117, 119, 123–125, 130, 142–143, **149**
as *Quakahkanumad* ("woman-who-prays-always"), 114
Duchesne, Pierre-François, 111
Duchesne, Rose-Euphrosine Perier, 111, 113
Durham, Fr. David, SJ, 79

Eaglin, Dave, **33**, 33–35, **51**
Eaglin, Jenny. *See* Hawkins, Jenny Eaglin Martin
Eaglin, Julia Ann, **33**, 33–34, **51**
Elder, Mother Rose, RSCJ, 22
enslaved people. *See* slavery
Erskine, Marjory, RSCJ, 77
Estevan, Fr., 101

"Fabiola" (play), 75
Feast of *Mater Admirabilis*, 55
Finn, Margaret Mary, RSCJ, 48
Fitzwilliam, Mother Mary, RSCJ, 79, 158–159
Flood, Great Flood of 1927, 61, 143–146
Fontenot, District Attorney Austin, 75

Gavan, Sr. Mary Lou, RSCJ, *vi*, 157
Gerard, Sister, 23
Gifts, giving opportunities, 163–164
glossary, 139–141
Goetz, Mother Josephine, RSCJ, 41, 47, 54
Gough, Ignatius, 34
*goûter* (snack, treat), 103, **103,** 132, 139

**172** *Index*

Grant, General Ulysses S., 41
Great Flood of 1927, 61, 143–146
Guidroz, Sr. Rose, RSCJ, 131, **131**, 152, 155, **155**, 156
Guidry, Peggy, **98**
Guillory, Sr. Tippy, RSCJ, 96

**H**aggarty, Sr. Carol, RSCJ, 63, 135, **135**, 160–161
Hamontree, Maggie, 130
Hardey, Mother Mary Anne Aloysia, RSCJ, 23, **35**, 39–40, 55, **118**, 118–119
Hawkins, Benjamin, Sr., 21, 33, **33, 51**
Hawkins, Francis (Frank, Jr.), 21, 31–33, **33, 51**
Hawkins, Frank, Sr., 21, 31–35, **33**, 46, **51**
Hawkins, Jenny Eaglin, 21, 31, **33**, 33–35, 46, **51**
"Her Son's Sweetheart" (play), 75
Hoffman, Sr. Margaret "Mike," RSCJ, 48, **50, 83**
Hubbell, Megan, 131
Hurricane Andrew, 135
Hurricane Audry, 143
Hurricane Gustav, 93, 95, **95**, 143
Hurricane Katrina, 66, **86**, 93, **94**, 96, 136, 143
Hurricane Laura, 96
Hurricane of September 14, 1823, 23
Hurricane Rita, 136, 143
*Hyacintha* (magic lantern show), 35
hymns, 147–148

**I**llinois Confederation (Native Americans), 113
Indians. *See* Native Americans

**J**eanmard, Bishop Jules B., 59, 75–76, 81
Jenkins, Sr. Mary Louise "Mamie," RSCJ, 132, **132**
Jouve, Euphrosine Aloysia, 123
Jouve, Jean-Joseph, 123
Jouve, Mother Aloysia Marguerite-Amélie, 36–37, 39, **39**, 40, 122–124, **123**, 157

**K**aram, Bonnie, 129
Karam, Sr. Rita, RSCJ, 129, **129**, 130, 160
Karam, Sr. Sharon, RSCJ, *vii*, 160–161
Karam, Tom, 129
Keyes, Louise, RSCJ, 147
Kondolf, Sr. Claire, RSCJ, 134, **134**, 135, 160

**L**a Société du Sacré Coeur de Jésus. *See* Religious of the Sacred Heart of Jesus
Ladies of the World, 36, 146

Lalonde, Una Bernadette. *See* Moreau, Una Bernadette Lalonde
Landry, Isabel, 131
Landry, Mother Carmelite, RSCJ, 22–23, 119–120, 157
Layton, Sr. Mary, *iv*, 13–15, **16**, 17, 23, **84**
*Le Rapide* (boat), 14, **16**
LeCompte, Mr. Ashton, 79
Lee, General Robert E., 41
*Les Loisirs de l'Abbeye* (memoir) (Perdrau), 54
Lévèque, Mother Louisa, 119, 123, 157
Lincoln, President Abraham, 142
Little, Sr. Maureen, RSCJ, 102
Lovallier, Louis, 24
Lynch, Mary Josephine, 74

**M**adonna of the Lily. *See Mater Admirabilis*
Makrina, Mother (abbess of Basilian Nuns of Minsk), 52
Manteau, Marguerite, 14
maps, **38, 60, 84**
Marheineke, Sr. Anna Mae, RSCJ, 150, **150**, 151
Maroney, Sarah, 132
Martin, 33, **33**, 34, **51**
Martinez, Mother Victoria Pizzaro, 40, 42–43, 46, 123–125, 157
Mary, Mother of God
  as Blessed Virgin, 34, 55–56, 120
  as Mary, the Immaculate Mother, 79
  as *Mater Admirabilis*
    consecration to, 149
    Feast of, 55, 103
    paintings of, 52–54, 110
    patron of Sacred Heart Schools, 55
    statue of, 79, **149**
  and St. John Berchmans, 116
  statue of, 104, **149**
*Mater Admirabilis* (painting) (Perdrau), 52–54, **53**
Mattern, Fr. E., SJ, 59
Maxwell, Sr. Susan, RSCJ, 83
McDuffie, Sr. Mathilde "Mac," RSCJ (St. Francis of Grand Coteau), **105**, 132–133, **133**, 163
McGlasson, Mrs. Karen, 66, **71**
Mélite, 33, **33**, 34, **51**
Memorare Hall, 63–64, **67**, 75, **76**, 104, 143
Millard, Doctor, 43
Mills, Sr. Alice, RSCJ, 133–134, **134**, 160
Miracle of Grand Coteau, 42–45, 116, 122, 125
Mme. X, 44–45
Montbrain, Louise, 17, 99
Moor, Paméla, 17
Moore, William, 24

Moran, Mother Mary Elizabeth, RSCJ, **122**, 122–123, 157–158
Moreau, John Herbert, Sr., 130
Moreau, Paula. *See* Chachere, Paula Moreau
Moreau, Sr. Barbara Ann, RSCJ, **130**, 130–131, 152–154, **154**, 163
Moreau, Una Bernadette Lalonde, 130
Moser, Theresa, RSCJ, 77
Mouton, Alexander, 99
Mouton, Msgr. Richard, 128
Mouton, Sr. Carolyn, **23**, 128, **128**, 160
Mouton, Sr. Odéide, RSCJ, 23, **23**, 128
Murinais, Mother de, 112
Murphy, Mother Anna Xavier, RSCJ, 18, 20–24, 26, 28, 35, 46, 55, 119–121, 142, 157

**N**achon, Fr. M., SJ, 43
Napoleon, 14, 111, 115
Native Americans, 112–115, 121
Nebbitt, Eliza "Lisa", **35**, 118–119
Nordmann, Sr. Lucie, RSCJ, *vii*

**O**din, Archbishop, 46–47
Ofelia (Mexican student), 110
Olivier, Fr., 30, 47
Order of the Holy Family, 48
Osiek, Sr. Carolyn, RSCJ, *vi*, 178
*Our Lady in the House of St. John* (painting) (Perdrau), 54

**P**apillion, Anna, 66
Papillion, Darrel J., 66
Papillion, Shirley, 66
Percy, Walker, 127
Perdrau, Joseph, 54
Perdrau, Pauline, RSCJ, 52, 54, **54**, 110, 177
Perier, Rose-Euphrosine. *See* Duchesne, Rose-Euphrosine Perier
Perier, Tante, 112
Pezolt, Colette, 77
Phillip (apostle), 111
Plauche, Sr. Antonia "Mother Plauche", "Sister Tony," RSCJ, 127–128, **128**, 160
poems, 150–151
Point, Fr. Nicholas, 29–30, **30**
Poiret, Félonise, 17
Pope John Paul II, 115, 130
Pope John XXIII, 82
Pope Leo XII, 52
Pope Leo XIII, 56, 142

Pope Pius IX, 41, 52, 54, 56
Pope Pius VI, 108
Pope Pius XI, 78, 110
Pope Pius XII, 75
Potawatomie (Native Americans), 114
prayers, 53, 147–149
Primary School, 83, 102–103, 134, 143

**Q**uakahkanumad ("woman-who-prays-always"). *See* Duchesne, Mother Rose Philippine, RSCJ
Quebedeau, Caroline, 137

**R**ambaud, Aloysia, 113–114
Ray, Fr. Sam Hill, 116
*Rebecca* (ship), 14, 114
recipes, 152–156
Religious of the Sacred Heart of Jesus (*La Société du Sacré Coeur de Jésus*)
    administrative leaders, 117–137; 157–161
    becoming a Religious, procedure, 162
    biographies, 107–115, 117–137
    and Jesuits, 29–30
    saints of. *See* Barat, St. Madeleine Sophie, RSCJ; Duchesne, Mother Rose Philippine, RSCJ
    slavery and, 17, 20–21, 26, 31–35, **33**, 37, 46, 50–51, **55**
    and Vatican II, **55**, 82–83, **82–83**, 87, 143, 162
Richardson, Samuel, 107
Rives, Mary Pat, RSCJ, 76–77, 160
Robin. *See* Blood, Catherine "Robin," RSCJ
Roosevelt, President Franklin Delano, 79–80
Rosary, The (Network of Sacred Heart Schools sister school), 55, 74, 76, **86**, 93, **94**, 129, 130, 135–136
Rosati, Bishop, 20
Rose of Lima (saint), 111
Roth, Sarah, 129
Rousseau, Gadrate, 17
Rousseau, Zelia, 17, 23, 99
Rouxel, Msgr., 62

**S**acred Heart Parochial School (now St. Ignatius Elementary School), 48
Saint Peter Claver School, 48, **49, 81, 83**
saints. *See* Barat, St. Madeleine Sophie, RSCJ; Berchmans, St. John; Duchesne, Mother Rose Philippine, RSCJ
Saizan, Sr. Claire, RSCJ, 126, **126**, 160, 163
Saunders, Mary B., 148
scholarships, 163

Schools of the Sacred Heart, 96
  *See also* Academy of the Sacred Heart - Grand Coteau; Berchmans Academy of the Sacred Heart; Rosary, The
Schwing, George, 24
Second Vatican Council. *See* Vatican II
Sentee, Mary
  *See also* Smith, Mrs. Charles (Mary Sentee)
    pupil, 17
Servaes, Dr. Anna (Laurie), *vi*, 61, 144, 178
Shannon, Mother Anna, RSCJ, 40–41, 47, 55, 124, 157
Sisters of the Holy Family, 48, 81, **81**
slavery
  and Academy/Religious of the Sacred Heart - Grand Coteau, 17, 20–21, 26, 31–35, **33**, 37, 46, 50–51, **51**
  and *Code Noir*, 31
  enslaved people
    buried in St. Charles Borromeo cemetery, 35
    and *Code Noir*, 31
    descendants in Grand Coteau, 46
    emancipation of, 46
    and Emancipation Proclamation, 51
    named on monument in cemetery, **51**
    named on plaque, **33**
    quarters for, 20, 26, **32**, 34
    and riots, 34
*Smile the Sun Around My Heart: The Collected Poems of Anna Mae Marheineke, RSCJ* (Marheineke), 150
Smith, Benjamin, 46
Smith, Blanche, 77
Smith, Charles, 13, 77, 93
Smith, Darlene (author of book), *vii*, 179, **179**
Smith, John, 77
Smith, Mrs. Charles (Mary Sentee), *iv*, 13–15, **16, 28,** 29, 31, 93, 117
Smith, Sr. Carmen Margaret, RSCJ, 126–127, **127,** 149
*Société du Sacré Coeur de Jésus. See* Religious of the Sacred Heart of Jesus
sources, *vi*, 165–166
*Sr. Mary Wilson's Attestation Concerning Her Miraculous Cure through the Intercession of St. John Berchmans* (Wilson), 42
St. Charles Borromeo Parish, 48, 50
St. Charles College, 29–30, **30,** 48, 61, 78, 145
St. Francis of Grand Coteau. *See* McDuffie, Sr. Mathilde "Mac," RSCJ

St. Ignatius Elementary School, 48
St. John Berchmans School for Boys. *See* Berchmans Academy of the Sacred Heart
St. Madeleine Sophie Barat. *See* Barat, St. Madeleine Sophie, RSCJ
St. Rose Philippine Duchesne. *See* Duchesne, Mother Rose Philippine, RSCJ

Tate, Bernice, **153**
Taylor, General Richard, 37
*The Society of the Sacred Heart in North America* (Callan), 37
Thensted, Fr. Cornelius, SJ, 48, **50,** 116
Thensted Center, 48, **50,** 82, **83, 105,** 131, 134, 177
Thompson, Mary Grace, 127
timeline, 142–143
Tommasini, Mother Maria Stanislas, RSCJ, 124, **125,** 126, 158
Tournély, Fr. Léonor François de, 108
Town, A. Hays, 63
Townsend, Sr. Katharine, RSCJ, *vi*
Trout, Ginny, 77
Trout, Lily, 77
Truman, President Harry, 80
"Two Naughty Old Ladies" (play), 75

Ulloa, Governor Antonio de, 31
Ursulines, 14, 114, 119–120, 123

Varin, Fr. Joseph Desiré, 108
Vatican II, **55,** 82–83, **82–83,** 87, 143, 162
Vialleton, Fr., 55
Vidaud, Louise de, 113–114
Villere, Sr. Anita "Nita," RSCJ, 128–129, **129,** 160
Virgil, 107

Wiley, A'Jani, 54
Williams, M., RSCJ, 148
Wilson, Mary, RSCJ, *vi*, 42, **42,** 43, **43, 45,** 116, 122–125, 136, 142
Wiltz, Lauran, 125

Xavier, Mother. *See* Murphy, Mother Anna Xavier, RSCJ

Yerger, Ella, 127

# Contact Information

### *To inquire about enrolling your child in The Academy of the Sacred Heart or Berchmans Academy...*

Schools of the Sacred Heart
Office of Admissions
P.O. Box 310
1821 Academy Road
Grand Coteau, LA 70541

Phone: (337) 662-7064
Fax: (337) 662-3011
Email: admissions@sshcoteau.org

Website: https://sshcoteau.org/academy/admissions/apply/

### *To inquire about scheduling a tour of St. John Berchmans Shrine or the Academy Museum...*

Schools of the Sacred Heart
P.O. Box 310
1821 Academy Road
Grand Coteau, LA 70541

Phone: (337) 662-5275
Fax: (337) 662-3011

Website: https://sshcoteau.org/academy/about/toursphoto-policy/

### *To inquire about becoming a member of the Society of the Sacred Heart...*

Society of the Sacred Heart
United States Province
4120 Forest Park Blvd.
St. Louis, MO 63108

Phone: (314) 652-1500
Fax: (314) 534-6800
Website: https://www.rscj.org

# Photo, Art, and Map Credits

Barry, Bonnie Taylor (Sunset, La.) – Cover, 5, 67, 73

Bell, Elizabeth (Lafayette, La.) – 60, 84

Blood, Catherine, RSCJ (Illustration of Philippine Duchesne's arrival in America) – 149

Claudel, Roger (Scott, La.) – 81

de la Herran, Pilar, RSCJ – 147

Izzo, Danny (*Nouveau Photeau*, Lafayette, La.) – 62

Jesuit Archives, U.S. Central & Southern Province, St. Louis, Mo. – 50

Nealis, Margaret Mary, RSCJ – 15

Perdrau, Pauline, RSCJ (Society of the Sacred Heart, Rome) – 53

Quebedeaux, Charles J. (Illustration of *Le Rapide*) – 16

Society of the Sacred Heart Archives, St. Louis, Mo. (Original Academy building) – 16

Stremel, Gary – 64, 66

Thensted Outreach Center, Grand Coteau, La. – 83

# Acknowledgements

A venture of this scope relies on the help of people who generously volunteer their services. I was blessed to have the assistance of several.

Great gratitude is due to Sr. Carolyn (Lyn) Osiek, RSCJ, and Sr. Mary Lou Gavan, RSCJ, the St. Louis archivists who gave me much-needed guidance and editing. They provided Sacred Heart information found only in the archives, including the extensive list of headmistresses and directors of the Academy. For all that, I am very grateful but especially for the moral support and encouragement Sr. Osiek gave me over the two years it took to complete this work.

Sections of the book were painstakingly translated by my colleague and language teacher at ASH, Dr. Laurie (Anna) Servaes. One particularly enjoyable part of this work was that we sometimes held our meetings at *La Madeleine* over lunch!

Language arts students under the guidance of ASH English teacher Roxanne Guillory wrote some of the profiles of the leading ladies of Grand Coteau, found in Chapter 20. Kudos to the **Class of 2022**: Allie Frey, Lillian Cain, Olivia Courville, and Maggie Hamontree; **Class of 2023**: Hannah Cheeran, Caroline Corley, Roisin Davoren, Megan Hubbell, Isabel Landry, Lillith McConnell, Sarah Roth, Eve Talbot, Mary Grace Thompson, and Ella Yerger; **Class of 2024**: Vivian Allie and Lauren Wiltz. Two of my former students, Christina Cain Popp and Aimee David Cotter, also helped with gathering and writing information for the sections on athletics and on continuing support of the Academy. Thanks to all these writers for their participation in this project. You made my task a little easier.

A former student of mine and the Director of the Shrine of St. John Berchmans, Caroline Richard, was invaluable since she took on the responsibility of gathering pictures and assisting with their placement in the book. The book wouldn't be as accurate without her help and expertise, especially her very careful fact-checking!

Irma Dillard, RSCJ, and Maureen Chicoine, RSCJ, provided insight, inspiration, and information during several stages of work on this book. I am grateful for their assistance.

The publishing staff at Acadian House Publishing in Lafayette, La., deserves much gratitude for their meticulous care and attention to detail during production. Trent Angers, the publisher, and his staffers, Allison Nassans and Madison Louviere, provided much-needed expertise in editing, placing photos and text, and designing the artistic elements of the book.

Most of all, I am so grateful to my family, especially my ever-so-patient husband, Norman; my daughter, Jessica Smith Cornay (Class of 1993); my granddaughters, Mary Adele and Clara, who think it's "cool" that their Mimi wrote a book; and my older sister, Jan Penka, who just would not let me give up.

# About the Author...

DARLENE SMITH is a retired school teacher who taught in Kansas and Louisiana for 40 years. Most of her teaching (1981-2012) was done at the Academy of the Sacred Heart in Grand Coteau, La., where she specialized in English, literature and Louisiana history.

After retiring from teaching, she worked in the Editorial Department of Acadian House Publishing in Lafayette, La., for six years as a writer, copy editor, proofreader and researcher.

She was educated in Catholic schools from First Grade until she was a junior in college. She earned a BA in English from Wichita State University, then a Master's in Gifted Education from the University of Southwestern Louisiana.

She and her husband, Norman Smith, live in Lafayette, La., and are the proud parents of a daughter, Jessica, who is a graduate of the Academy where Darlene taught for 31 years.

# Books about
# GRAND COTEAU
From
## Acadian House Publishing

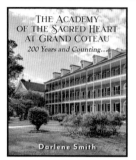

### The Academy of the Sacred Heart at Grand Coteau
*200 Years and Counting...*

A 176-page hardcover book that tells the 200-year history of the Academy of the Sacred Heart at Grand Coteau, La. Published in the school's Bicentennial year, the book notes that this all-girls Catholic educational institution, founded in 1821, is the longest continuously running Sacred Heart school in the world. The text takes the reader through the nuns' early struggles to establish the school, then the antebellum years, the Civil War, the Great Flood of 1927, and World War II. Also, the Miracle of Grand Coteau, the founding of the College of the Sacred Heart, and the traditions, customs and standards that make the school unique. It includes hymns, prayers, poems, recipes, and a timeline of key events. Illustrated with maps, paintings, and scores of historical and contemporary photos. (Author: Darlene Smith; ISBN: 1-7352641-1-3; Price: $50.00)

### Grand Coteau
*The Holy Land of South Louisiana*

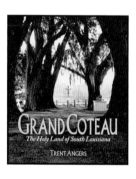

A 176-page hardcover book that captures the spirit of one of the truly holy places in North America. It is a town of mystery, with well-established ties to the supernatural, including the famous Miracle of Grand Coteau. Brought to life by dozens of exceptional color photographs, the book focuses on the town's major religious institutions: The Academy of the Sacred Heart, Our Lady of the Oaks Retreat House and St. Charles College/Jesuit Novitiate. The book explores not only the history of these three institutions but also the substance of their teachings. (Author: Trent Angers. ISBN: 0-925417-47-5. Price: $44.95)

### A Place Set Apart

A 176-page hardcover book about **Our Lady of the Oaks Jesuit Retreat House** – a place of peace and beauty in Grand Coteau, La., where men and women go to pray and refresh body and soul. The book features the history of the facility and an explanation of its place in the worldwide retreat movment. It contains lots of photos, a prayer section, interviews with retreatants, a definition of the Spiritual Exercises of St. Ignatius, and mini-bios of the Jesuit retreat directors who have served here over the years. (Editor: Trent Angers. ISBN: 0-9995884-7-8. Price: $32.50)

**TO ORDER,** list the books you wish to purchase along with the corresponding cost of each. Add $4 per book for shipping & handling. Louisiana residents add 8% tax to the cost of the books. Mail your order and check or credit card authorization (VISA/MC/AmEx) to: Acadian House Publishing, Dept. ASH, P.O. Box 52247, Lafayette, LA 70505. Or call (800) 850-8851. To order online, go to www.acadianhouse.com.

The book on the Academy of the Sacred Heart can also be ordered directly from the Academy by calling (337) 662-5275.